The First Real Kitchen Cookbook

The

FIRST REAL KITCHEN

COOKBOOK

RECIPES & TIPS FOR NEW COOKS

MEGAN & JILL CARLE

PHOTOGRAPHS BY SHERI GIBLIN

CHRONICLE BOOKS

SAN FRANCISCO

Library of Congress Cataloging-in-Publication Data:
Carle, Megan.
    First Real Kitchen Cookbook : recipes and tips for new cooks /
Megan & Jill Carle ; photography by Sheri Giblin
        p. cm.
    ISBN 978-0-8118-7810-4
1. Cooking. 2. Youth—Nutrition. I. Carle, Jill. II. Giblin, Sheri. III. Title.

    TX714.C3731545 2011
    641.5—dc22

                                                    2010023927

Manufactured in China

Designed by Anne Donnard
Prop styling by Christine Wolheim
Food styling by Erin Quon

The publisher thanks Falletti Foods in San Francisco for generously
providing the filming location for the videos that appear in *The First
Real Kitchen Cookbook* mobile phone and ebook applications.

10 9 8 7 6 5 4 3 2 1

Chronicle Books LLC
680 Second Street
San Francisco, CA 94107
www.chroniclebooks.com

ACKNOWLEDGMENTS

As always, our thanks to our editor, Lorena Jones, who continues to believe in our projects, puts up with our nonsense, and always seems to get it, even when we aren't sure what we're saying. You keep us energized and make the whole thing more fun.

To our friend Karen Ewart, cook extraordinaire and generally nice person to be around. We couldn't have finished on time without you. You came, you cooked, you conquered!

Many thanks to our ace team of taste testers. You showed up week after week and tried every dish, even when it looked questionable. Your input was invaluable.

And last on the list, but first in our hearts: Dad, Andrew, and Michi. We thank you for putting up with us and all of our messes and for keeping us from going completely over the edge.

TABLE OF CONTENTS

Chapter 4: CHICKEN

Chapter 5: BEEF

Chapter 6: PORK

continued

Chapter 7: DESSERTS

INTRODUCTION

You're finally out of college and in a real place of your own, or at least one that doesn't make your parents shudder the first time they see it. You feel like a grown-up because your bed actually has a frame instead of the mattress sitting right on the floor. You've looked at new furniture, realized how much it costs, and bought new throw pillows for the old stuff, figuring that will spruce it up for now. And you have a real kitchen—including a stove with four working burners, a refrigerator with all the shelves, and a countertop that was actually made sometime in this century! So now what do you do with it? We're glad you asked, because we can help you with that. (The kitchen part anyway. For the decorating . . . you're on your own.)

We both started helping our mom in the kitchen when we were about three years old. Messing around is probably a better way to say it, though, since we probably weren't any help and certainly made plenty of messes. We both love cooking and spent a lot of time in the kitchen over the years, working on our creations. We are not professional chefs and don't pretend to be. They work way too hard. We just like to cook and are pretty good at it, if we do say so ourselves. Through many years of experimenting, we've learned what works and what doesn't and, between the two of us, have come up with a large and varied repertoire of dishes. We have completely different tastes in food; one of us leans toward comfort foods—whether they are American or other ethnicities—while the other loves any kind of ethnic foods, the hotter the better. For you, that means a lot of different choices in our book.

Although there are a wide variety of recipes, we only used ingredients you can get at a regular grocery store. We're not going to make you run to six different ethnic markets trying to find unusual ingredients. And when we use pricier ingredients, we try to give you cheaper alternatives. We understand the whole budget thing very well. We each have one roommate and neither one of us spends more than $200 a month on groceries for both people. We do eat dinner out once or twice a week, but we eat breakfast at home and usually take our lunches to work. It's not that we try that hard to stay on a budget; being thrifty just seems to be in our genes. You'll notice that most of the recipes serve four people. Even though we're cooking for only two, we make the meals for four, and the leftovers become the next day's lunch. It's easy to spend a lot each day on lunch out, so bringing it from home saves a ton of money. We also stock up when things are on sale. You can get canned tomatoes or beans at less than half of their regular price when they go on sale. You can bet when they do we're buying ten or twelve cans. They last a long time, and we know we'll use them. You can also save a lot of money that way on meat. When it's on sale, it's often about one third of the regular price. Buy the family pack, cut it into the sizes you usually use, individually wrap them in plastic wrap/cling film, and freeze. (We do this with everything except whole chickens because they take up too much space in the freezer.) The bonus is you don't have to run to the store all the time. If you've got some meat in the freezer, some canned goods, and a fresh veggie or two, you can always come up with a good meal.

We make quite a few (in our view) common-sense assumptions about cooking practices and ingredients. Wash your fruits and vegetables before eating or cooking with them. Don't touch goopy, raw chicken and then touch your raw vegetables. Wash your hands after touching raw meats. It's not rocket science. You've been hearing it for years from your mom, so pay attention to her advice! There are a few other assumptions that we make that may not seem as blatantly obvious as proper hygiene, like vegetable size. If we specify a small or large onion in a recipe, we mean a small or large onion. If we don't specify, we mean a medium onion. When we say butter, we mean butter in the generic sense. If you want to use salted or unsalted butter or (gasp!) margarine, go for it. There will not be an earth-shattering difference in the taste of your food. We use salted butter because it's what we're used to. The same goes for mayonnaise, milk, sour cream, etc.

Use what you use normally, unless you're baking; then go for full-fat everything, which is probably why dessert is so delicious.

You'll notice that we include metric measurements and celsius temperature equivalents. (We didn't want our European friends left out.) Make sure you're following the measurements and temperatures that apply.

Neither one of us has a gourmet kitchen; it just seems that way compared to our last kitchen. We rented a place together in college that had a four-burner stove so small that a frying pan took up two burners, the oven wouldn't fit anything larger than a 9-by-13-in/23-by-32-cm pan, and it literally had 2 ft/61 cm of counter space. After that, anything seems spacious. If you're like us, you're still using your pots and pans from college . . . at least the ones that still have handles. As you can afford it, think about upgrading to a few better pieces. Start with a good-quality frying pan and saucepan with metal handles so they can also go in the oven. Buy the larger ones first. You can cook a small amount of food in a large pan, but you can't cook a large amount of food in a small pan. You can add the smaller ones later. Pans like that aren't cheap, but they'll last forever. You can lessen the blow a little by shopping around. We have found them at outlet stores for about half of the regular price. One large and one small nonstick pan also come in handy. We buy them at a discount store so we don't feel as bad about replacing them every couple of years when they get scratched. You should have a couple of 9-by-13-in/23-by-32-cm baking dishes and a couple of baking sheets/trays. You don't have to break the bank on those; just make sure they are thick enough so they don't bend. And remember: If you have a small oven, measure how wide it is; the baking sheets with the handles on the sides might be too long. We know that from experience. A set of stacking bowls, a colander, cutting board, measuring cups, measuring spoons, vegetable peeler, a blender, and a can opener are also necessities. You can get away with just a few utensils: a metal spatula, plastic spatula for nonstick pans, rubber scraper, large spoon, large slotted spoon, and a few decent knives. If you already have those things, you can move on to the helpful, but not necessary items such as a box grater, garlic press, whisk, strainer, meat thermometer, grill/barbecue pan, and a pastry brush. With the exception of the pots and pans, none of those items is very expensive, and they are fun to buy. Or maybe that's just us. It's kind of ridiculous how excited we can get over a new set of stacking bowls or a garlic press.

Once you learn the basics, you can begin to adjust things to your taste. Don't worry; we won't be offended. The idea isn't to learn to cook what we like—it's to learn to cook what you like. If this book helps you learn to cook without a recipe, we consider our job more than done. Obviously, that's a stretch since we ourselves still use recipes (some of us more than others . . . cough, cough, JILL, cough). But, our goal is for you to figure out what you like and realize that most recipes are not immovable works of art but interpretations of various dishes. So why shouldn't you be able to have your own interpretation? Something you've made "just right" for you? So give it a whirl and see what you come up with. We suggest starting with a basic recipe and modifying just a couple things to start. Maybe add a different spice, or a new vegetable. Try to keep the proportions similar so you don't end up with way too many vegetables for the amount of sauce in a stir-fry, or a beef curry that's swimming in coconut milk. Eventually, you'll feel comfortable changing things around or even making up your own recipes. If it's awful, then you know not to do it that way in the future! Either way it won't be that bad. In fact, it might be even more delicious than you imagined.

Chapter

VEGETABLES

Vegetables aren't just for vegetarians. They are a necessity in cooking because they add flavor, color, and texture. Changing the vegetables, or merely how you cook them, can completely change the flavor of a dish. When vegetables are cooked in a liquid, as in soups or stews, they soften and give the liquid some of their flavor and, with longer cooking times, they can pick up a little flavor from the other vegetables with which they are cooked. When sautéed, vegetables will keep their own flavor and are generally cooked to what is called "tender-crisp," meaning they are not completely soft. Roasted vegetables are cooked until tender, but because there is no liquid, the flavor intensifies and the sugars caramelize, making them sweeter. None of these methods is better than the others; they are just used in different situations.

Maneuvering your way through the produce department doesn't need to be intimidating, just look for three things: bright color for the vegetable type, leaves that are green and crisp, and firmness with no soft spots. Vegetables that are past their prime aren't worth buying; as they age, they lose flavor and often get bitter. It is better to substitute a different vegetable than to use an inferior one. Think about what the vegetable adds to the dish—it could be flavor, texture, or color (or all three)—and find something that would provide the same. The following vegetables are grouped by similar items. In most cases these can be substituted for each other.

MUSHROOMS

Button or white mushrooms are the most common, mildest, and least expensive. Use these when a recipe calls for mushrooms without listing a type. Portobellos are large, meaty, and full flavored. Cremini/brown mushrooms (sometimes called baby portobellos) are smaller than four inches in diameter. They are not as firm as larger portobellos but are full flavored.

Fresh shiitake mushrooms have a meaty, buttery flavor, but when dried they get more smoky. Wood ear and oyster mushrooms are very mild and are usually used for texture rather than flavor. Shiitake, wood ear, and oyster mushrooms often need to be purchased dry and must be reconstituted in hot water for 30 minutes.

SWEET PEPPERS/CAPSICUMS

Green bell peppers/capsicums are picked earlier and have a sharper flavor than those of other colors. Red, yellow, orange, white, and purple varieties are all similar enough in flavor to be interchangeable. You can often get packages of mixed colored assortments that are good if you want different colors in smaller amounts.

HOT PEPPERS/CHILLIS

Pasillas and Anaheims are at the lowest end of the heat scale and are great for stuffing. Hatch green chiles are usually hotter than the Anaheims, but they are also good for stuffing or for roasting and using for salsa or stew.

Serranos and jalapeños are good for salsas or for spicing up a dish, but beware: Serranos are five times hotter than jalapeños.

Habaneros are the hottest readily available variety. Use with caution!

ROOT VEGETABLES

Parsnips look like a white carrot and have a mild, sweet flavor that is a cross between a carrot and a potato. Turnips have a similar flavor, but with a sharp bite to it. A rutabaga/swede is like a turnip on steroids. It's more of everything: bigger, sharper, and more bitter. These root vegetables are all similar enough in flavor to be interchangeable in soups or stews, but different enough to be combined in a roasted vegetable dish without being boring.

Beets/beetroots are the sweetest of the root vegetables. They are great roasted or pickled but are seldom used in stews because they turn the whole dish red. For that matter, they turn your hands, cutting board, and pretty much everything else they touch red, too.

Russet potatoes are starchy, making them great for baking or mashing. Red potatoes have less starch and are good for boiling or salads because they hold their shape. Yukon golds and fingerlings are considered all-purpose. They are great for roasting, pan frying, and using in soups and stews but aren't as good as russets for baking or mashing.

Sweet onions include Vidalia, Walla Walla, or Maui. They are usually only available April to August and are interchangeable.

Dry onions include red, yellow (sometimes called brown), and white, which are all available year-round. Don't confuse these with dried (dehydrated) minced onion. Dry onions are the onions you use all the time; they're just categorized as dry because of the layers of dry, papery skin on the outside. Yellow onions are the most pungent and are best when cooked. White onions are slightly sweeter than yellows, but they can be used interchangeably. Red onions are the most mellow of this group and are best raw or barely cooked, such as grilled or in a quick stir-fry. Longer cooking washes out the great red-purple color.

Shallots are small dry onions, but have a more delicate garlicky flavor.

Leeks have a mild, slightly sweet flavor, but make sure to clean them well. Dirt usually gets between the layers when they're growing.

Scallions and green/spring onions are technically different species, but they can be used interchangeably.

TOMATOES

There is nothing like a sweet, flavorful, home-grown tomato. Unfortunately that is too true. There is nothing like them in the supermarket. In the summer months, you can get good tomatoes at farmers' markets or farm stands if they have them in your area. If none of those choices is available, try the vine-ripened tomatoes at grocery stores. They're usually pretty good, but they can be expensive. If they are too rich for your budget, stick with Roma tomatoes (also called plum tomatoes). They are the most consistent and are generally less expensive than the other types.

GREENS

Spinach is the most popular and most tender of the greens. It can be eaten raw or sautéed lightly. Collard greens, red or Swiss chard, and mustard greens are a little more bitter and require longer cooking times. If you buy them in bunches (rather than bags), make sure to wash them. And then wash them again because they can be covered in really fine sand. There's nothing worse than gritty greens.

CABBAGE

Green and red cabbage have similar flavors and are interchangeable when raw, but when cooking red cabbage you need to add acid (vinegar or lemon juice) or it turns a weird blue color. Savoy cabbage grows in heads like green cabbage, but the leaves have lacy ridges. Savoy can be used interchangeably with green cabbage. Napa cabbage (also called Chinese cabbage) is pale green and comes in heads that look more like romaine/Cos lettuce. It is good in salad and stir-fry. Bok choy comes in large heads with dark green leafy ends. The stalk and the leafy ends are both commonly used in stir-fry. Baby bok choy can be used interchangeably with bok choy, but it's usually more expensive because it's so cute. Okay, that may not be why—but it *is* really cute.

SQUASH/COURGETTES

Summer squash/courgettes, such as zucchini and yellow squash, are thin skinned and easily bruised. They are great for grilling or sautéing.

Winter squash such as butternut and acorn are great baked, roasted, or in soups. Spaghetti squash is also a winter squash but is handled differently. It can be baked in the oven or cooked in the microwave, and then the threads are peeled out with a fork. It looks kind of weird, but it's pretty delicious.

VEGETABLE USES

STIR-FRIED

GRILLED

ROASTED
(OVEN)

STEWED
(SOUPS/STEWS)

MUSHROOMS
CARROTS
GREEN/SPRING ONIONS

CABBAGE

HOT PEPPERS/CHILLIS
SWEET PEPPERS/
CAPSICUMS

SWEET ONIONS

SWEET POTATOES
BEETS/BEETROOTS
SPAGHETTI SQUASH

CELERY

DRY ONIONS
ZUCCHINI/COURGETTES
YELLOW SQUASH

PORTOBELLOS
SWEET POTATOES

PARSNIPS
RUTABAGAS/SWEDES
TURNIPS
BUTTERNUT SQUASH
ACORN SQUASH

POTATOES

TOMATOES

MUSHROOMS
CARROTS
LEEKS

GRILLED SUMMER VEGETABLES
WITH BALSAMIC VINAIGRETTE

Megan

This is an incredibly versatile dish that screams summer. You can eat it hot or cold, as a main dish as-is, on top of a baked potato, as a side dish with any kind of grilled meat or fish, on top of a salad, with tortillas for fajitas, or even tossed with cooked pasta for a quick pasta salad. With that many choices, you can make a big batch and use the leftovers all week.

1 clove garlic

2 tbsp olive oil, plus extra for brushing the vegetables

2 tbsp balsamic vinegar

1 tsp brown mustard

1 tsp honey

Salt and pepper

1 large eggplant/aubergine

2 yellow squash/yellow courgettes

2 zucchini/courgettes

1 red onion

1 red bell pepper/capsicum

1 yellow bell pepper/capsicum

Peel and finely chop the garlic. Put the garlic, 2 tbsp olive oil, vinegar, mustard, and honey in a small bowl and stir until combined. Season with salt and pepper, and set aside.

Stem the eggplant/aubergine and cut it into lengthwise slices ½ in/12 mm thick. Stem the yellow squash/yellow courgette and zucchini/courgette and cut them in half lengthwise. Peel the onion and cut it into slices ¼ in/6 mm thick. Halve and seed the red and yellow bell peppers/capsicums.

Preheat a grill/barbecue or grill pan on high.

Brush the vegetables with oil (or coat with cooking spray) and sprinkle with salt and pepper. Put the vegetables on the grill/barbecue and cook, turning occasionally, for 10 to 15 minutes, or until fork tender. (The zucchini/courgette, squash, and eggplant/aubergine will take less time than the onion and peppers/capsicums.) Remove the vegetables from the grill/barbecue and cut them into pieces 1 in/2.5 cm long. Toss with the vinaigrette, season with salt and pepper, and serve immediately.

On the Lighter Side

This is the ultimate low-calorie dish. One serving clocks in at right around 150 calories. It also has more than 4 g of fiber, almost 3 g of protein, and only 7 g of fat and 20 g of carbs. Delicious and healthful—it's almost too much to ask for.

ROASTED ROOT VEGETABLES WITH COUSCOUS SERVES 4

Megan

This North African–inspired combination of colorful root vegetables looks beautiful and has a surprising combination of sweet and spicy flavors. You can serve it as a meal with the couscous or as a side dish without. Either way, it's delicious. I guarantee that once you try this dish you'll make it again and again.

1 sweet potato

1 lb/455 g red beets/beetroots

1 lb/455 g parsnips

3 carrots

3 tbsp olive oil

3 tbsp honey

2 tsp ground cumin

1 tsp salt

½ tsp cayenne pepper

1 large onion

2 tbsp butter

½ cup/65 g pine nuts

½ cup/85 g raisins

1 tsp ground cinnamon

2 cups/480 ml chicken or vegetable broth

1 cup/180 g couscous

Preheat the oven to 450°F/230°C/gas mark 8.

Peel the sweet potato, beets/beetroots, and parsnips and cut into chunks ¾ to 1 in/2 to 2.5 cm long. Peel the carrots and cut into pieces 1 in/2.5 cm long.

Put the olive oil, honey, cumin, salt, and cayenne in a small bowl and stir until combined. Put the sweet potato, parsnips, and carrots on one side of a baking sheet/tray and the beets/beetroots on the other side, leaving a few inches between them. (The latter bleed while they cook and will turn the other vegetables red.) Drizzle the honey mixture over the vegetables and toss them separately to completely coat. Bake for 30 minutes, or until the vegetables are golden brown and tender.

Peel, halve, and thinly slice the onion. Melt the butter in a medium frying pan over medium heat. Add the onion and cook, stirring occasionally, for 12 minutes, or until golden brown. Add the pine nuts and raisins and cook for 2 minutes. Stir in the cinnamon and remove from the heat.

Bring the broth to a boil in a medium saucepan and stir in the couscous. Remove from the heat, cover, and let stand 5 minutes. Fluff with a fork and keep warm.

Put some of the couscous on each plate and top with some of the roasted vegetables. Spoon the onion mixture on top of the vegetables and serve immediately.

Lingo

Chopping and dicing are not the same thing. When a recipe says **chop**, it means it doesn't matter what shape the pieces are, but **dice** means a more precise and consistent size and shape. We give you measurements when something should be cut to a certain size, but not everyone is as nice as we are. Seeing words like **baton** and **julienne** can throw you for a loop, so here's a quick translation:

Julienne: ⅛ by ⅛ by 2 in/3 mm by 3 mm by 5 cm

Allumette (also called matchstick): ¼ by ¼ by 2 in/6 mm by 6 mm by 5 cm

Baton: ½ by ½ by 2 in/12 mm by 12 mm by 5 cm

Brunoise: ⅛ in/3 mm cubes

Small dice: ¼ in/6 mm cubes

Medium dice: ½ in/12 mm cubes

Large dice: ¾ in/2 cm cubes

ROASTED BRUSSELS SPROUTS WITH BACON

Megan

Brussels sprouts are not only bite-size and cute, they only need a couple of ingredients to make them a mighty tasty, vitamin-packed side dish! These are the perfect accompaniment to a roast, meatloaf, or chicken when you already have the oven going. If you've never been a Brussels sprouts fan, you should give these a try. Roasting makes them a little crispy and brings out a whole different flavor. Besides, with this much bacon/streaky bacon on them, how can they be bad?

1 small onion

1½ to 2 lb/680 to 910 g fresh Brussels sprouts

8 oz/225 g bacon/streaky bacon

Salt and pepper

2 tbsp butter, melted

1 tbsp cider vinegar

½ tsp ground nutmeg

Preheat the oven to 350°F/180°C /gas 4.

Peel the onion and chop it into pieces ½ in/12 mm thick. Trim the stems of the Brussels sprouts, remove any dark leaves, and cut each in half through the core.

Cut the bacon into strips ½ in/12 mm wide. Put them in a large frying pan over medium-high heat and cook, stirring occasionally, for 10 minutes, or until crisp. Remove from the pan with a slotted spoon and drain on paper towels/absorbent paper. Add the onion to the pan and cook for 5 minutes, or until translucent. Add the Brussels sprouts to the pan and stir until coated. Put the mixture on a baking sheet/tray in a single layer and season with salt and pepper. Bake for 35 minutes, or until the Brussels sprouts are tender.

Place the Brussels sprouts in a bowl, add the melted butter, vinegar, nutmeg, and bacon, and stir until combined. Serve immediately.

Ingredient Info

There are zillions of types of vinegar on the market today, but we try to limit ourselves to just a few. We generally have either rice wine or white wine vinegars and red wine, cider, and balsamic vinegars in the cabinet. They all are good for cooking or vinaigrettes; it just depends on the flavor you want. Rice or white wine vinegars are very mild and give you the sharpness of vinegar without extra flavor. Red wine vinegar tastes like, well, vinegary red wine. Cider vinegar has a slightly sweet apple flavor, and balsamic has a rich, deep, slightly sweet flavor.

SPICY STIR-FRIED VEGETABLES

Megan

The epitome of fast and easy, this recipe is great for a quick meal when you want to eat right now. In the time it takes to cook the rice, you can have the vegetables cut, cooked, and ready to eat. It doesn't get much easier than that. You can make this with the vegetables we suggest or whatever you have in your refrigerator or freezer: fresh or frozen veggies and any type of meat will all work well.

1 cup/215 g dry white rice

2½ cups/600 ml water

¼ cup/60 ml soy sauce

2 tbsp sugar

1 tbsp cornstarch/cornflour

1 tbsp Asian chili paste

8 oz/230 g fresh mushrooms

1 red bell pepper/capsicum

1 bunch green/spring onions (about 6)

1½ cups/100 g snow peas

One 5-oz/140-g can bamboo shoots

3 cloves garlic

1 tbsp canola oil

1 tbsp grated peeled fresh ginger

1 tbsp finely chopped fresh cilantro/coriander

⅔ cup/75 g roasted cashews

Put the rice and 2¼ cups/540 ml of the water in a small saucepan and bring to a boil. Cover and cook over medium-low heat for 20 minutes, or until the rice is tender.

Meanwhile, combine the remaining ¼ cup/60 ml water, the soy sauce, sugar, cornstarch/cornflour, and chili paste in a small bowl and set aside.

Remove the stem ends from the mushrooms and thinly slice. Halve, seed, and cut the red bell pepper/capsicum into strips ¼ in/6 mm wide. Thinly slice the white and light green parts of the green/spring onions. Remove the strings from the pea pods (see below). Drain the bamboo shoots. Peel and finely chop the garlic.

Put the canola oil in a large frying pan over medium-high heat. Add the mushrooms and bell pepper/capsicum and cook for 5 minutes, or until the mushrooms just begin to soften. Add the green/spring onions and pea pods and cook, stirring occasionally, for 3 minutes, or until the pea pods are bright green, but still crisp. Add the garlic and ginger to the pan and cook, stirring constantly, for 30 seconds. Stir the soy sauce mixture and add it to the pan. Cook, stirring constantly, for 2 minutes, or until the sauce has thickened and the vegetables are cooked tender-crisp.

Place some of the rice on each plate and top with some of the vegetables. Sprinkle with the cilantro/coriander and cashews and serve immediately.

> ## Ingredient Info

Pea pods contain a string that begins at the stem and runs down the straight side of the pod. To remove the string, grasp the pea pod with your thumb and index finger just below the stem; gently press your thumbnail into the pea pod breaking off the stem, but leaving the string attached. Then just pull the string down the pea pod to remove it. Don't worry if all of the string doesn't come off. If it's thick enough to be bothersome, it will come off.

BRAISED COLLARD GREENS
WITH CREAMY POLENTA

Jill

Here's the ultimate Southern comfort food. Collard greens are best if they are slow-braised with some sweetness to offset their slight bitterness. I like to use apple juice because I think it goes well with the bacon/streaky bacon, but the greens are also good using water and a couple tablespoons of brown sugar. I suggest by the title to serve them with creamy polenta, but the reality is I usually use cornmeal. It is ground a little finer than polenta, but it has the exact same flavor, it cooks faster, and it's about half the cost.

COLLARD GREENS

1 lb/455 g fresh collard greens

4 slices bacon/streaky bacon

1 small onion

2 cups/480 ml apple juice

Salt and pepper

POLENTA

½ tsp salt

1 cup/140 g polenta or cornmeal

To prepare the collard greens: Remove the stems from the collard greens and roughly chop the leaves. Cut the bacon into pieces 1 in/2.5 cm long. Peel the onion and cut it into pieces ½ in/12 mm long.

Put the bacon in a stockpot and cook over medium heat for 5 minutes, or until a little of the fat is rendered (has cooked out of the bacon and collected in the pan). Add the onion and cook for 10 minutes, or until the bacon is brown and starting to get crisp. Drain off the fat and add the collard greens and apple juice. Cook over medium-low heat, stirring occasionally, for 45 minutes, or until very soft and most of the liquid is reduced. Season with salt and pepper.

To prepare the polenta: Bring 3 cups/720 ml water and the salt to a boil. Slowly stir in the polenta and cook, stirring frequently, for 15 to 20 minutes, or until smooth and creamy (cook for 6 to 7 minutes for cornmeal).

Spoon some of the polenta onto each plate, top with the collard greens, and serve immediately.

CHILES RELLENOS WITH MEXICAN RICE

Jill

This is our version of Chile Rellenos, which are a mystery to make for most people even though nearly every Mexican restaurant serves them. We simplified it by skipping the battering and frying and just baking them. This dish is not hard to make, but it is a little bit involved. What that really means is there are a fair amount of dishes to wash when you're finished. Fortunately, everything can be made ahead of time and refrigerated for up to one day. Then you can bake the Rellenos and reheat the rice and sauce just prior to serving. If the idea of roasting is too much for you, use eight canned whole chiles. All the heat in this dish is in the sauce; if you aren't a fan of spicy food, just use one chipotle in the sauce.

SAUCE

1 small onion

2 cloves garlic

4 Roma tomatoes

2 tbsp olive oil

2 chipotle peppers in adobo sauce

Salt and pepper

CHILES RELLENOS AND RICE

8 fresh Anaheim or 4 pasilla peppers/ chillis

2 onions

1 red bell pepper/capsicum

2 tbsp canola oil

1½ tsp ground cumin

2 cups/475 ml water

One 15-oz/430-g can diced tomatoes, with juices reserved

1 cup/215 g dry white rice

1 tsp chile powder

1 tsp salt

½ tsp black pepper

One 15-oz/430-g can black beans

2 cups/230 g shredded Monterey Jack or Mexican-style cheese

½ cup/120 ml sour cream

¼ cup/10 g chopped cilantro/ fresh coriander

To prepare the sauce: Peel and coarsely chop the onion and garlic. Roughly chop the tomatoes.

Heat the olive oil in a medium frying pan over high heat for 1 minute, or until it just begins to smoke. Add the tomatoes, onion, and garlic and cook, stirring occasionally, for 8 to 10 minutes, or until the onion is browned on the edges. Put the mixture in the blender, add the chipotles and puree until smooth. Season with salt and pepper and keep warm.

To prepare the chiles rellenos and rice: Place the Anaheims directly on the burner of a gas stove or under the broiler of an electric stove. Cook for 10 minutes, turning occasionally with tongs, until almost completely black on all sides. Put them in a bowl, cover tightly with plastic wrap/cling film, and let stand for 10 minutes. Scrape the skin from the flesh with the side of a knife, cut off the tops, and remove the seeds.

Peel the onions and chop into pieces ½ in/12 mm long. Halve, seed, and chop the bell pepper/capsicum into pieces ¼ in/6 mm.

Put the canola oil in a large frying pan and add the onions and bell pepper/capsicum. Cook, stirring occasionally, for 10 minutes, or until the onions are soft. Add the cumin and stir until combined. Remove ½ cup/120 ml of the onion mixture and put it in a bowl for later use. Add the water, diced tomatoes with the juice, rice, chile powder, and salt and pepper to the remaining onions and bring to a boil. Reduce to low heat and cook for 20 minutes, or until the rice is tender.

(continued)

Preheat the oven to 350°F/175°C/gas mark 4.

Meanwhile, drain the beans and add to the bowl with the reserved onions. Lightly mash some of the beans with a potato masher or fork, leaving some of them whole. Add the cheese, sour cream, and cilantro/fresh coriander and stir until completely combined. Hold one of the roasted peppers/chillis upright and put small spoonfuls of the bean mixture inside, pressing gently on the filling to completely fill the cavity, but being careful not to tear it. Repeat with the remaining peppers/chillis and filling. Put them in an 8-in/20-cm square baking dish and bake for 30 minutes, or until the filling just begins to melt out of the cut ends.

Place two rellenos on each plate and top with some of the sauce. Spoon some of the rice alongside the sauce and serve immediately.

Ingredient Info

All types of rice start as brown rice. Once the bran is removed, it becomes white rice. There aren't many choices for brown rice; most stores carry only long or medium grain. The selection of white rice is substantially larger. Generally the shorter the grain the more starch it contains. The starchier medium-grain rice is used for dishes such as sushi or risotto where the extra starch is beneficial. Because it contains less starch, long-grain rice is fluffier, particularly if it is parboiled (also called converted). Parboiling removes even more of the starch. Jasmine and basmati rice are aromatic rices that are similar in flavor. We generally use jasmine because it is usually the cheaper of the two. When a recipe calls for just "rice," we usually use either long-grain brown or parboiled white rice. Our cooking times are for white rice; for brown rice, increase the cooking time by approximately 15 minutes.

SPLIT PEA SOUP WITH HAM

Jill

I used a ham/gammon steak for this recipe, but you could use a ham bone from the butcher. Just put the bone in at the beginning and leave it in for the first hour. Then pull out the bone to cool slightly, remove the meat, and stir the pieces into the soup. Any leftover soup can be refrigerated for up to a week or frozen for several months.

2 carrots

1 small onion

1 lb/455 g dried split peas

2 bay leaves

3 qt/2.8 L water

Salt and pepper

1 lb/455 g ham/gammon steak

Peel the carrots and onion, cut into pieces ½ in/12 mm thick, and put them into a large saucepan. Add the peas, bay leaves, and the water and season with salt and pepper. Bring to a boil and simmer over medium-low heat, stirring occasionally, for 1 hour, or until the split peas are soft and just starting to break down.

`Cut the ham/gammon into bite-size pieces and add them to the pan. Cook, stirring occasionally, for 1 hour more, or until the peas break down completely. Season with salt and pepper and serve immediately.

On a Budget

Throughout the book, we give you tips when leftovers can be frozen. Sometimes I use resealable bags, but for something like this soup I use empty sour cream containers or the plastic containers that lunch meats come in. They hold just enough for one person and, most important, they're free. Do yourself a favor though and stick a piece of masking tape on the containers identifying what's inside. There's nothing worse than thinking you're grabbing soup and finding out at lunchtime that it's marinara sauce. When you go to reheat the contents, transfer to a ceramic or glass dish before microwaving; you can store leftovers in plastic, but reheating in them can cause the container to deteriorate and leach particulates into your food.

POTATO-LEEK SOUP

Jill

This soup has a very delicate flavor with an amazing silky texture. And it takes less than thirty minutes to prepare! You can serve it as a first course or add a loaf of crusty bread and make it a meal. Either way, it's delicious.

1 lb/455 g leeks

¼ cup/55 g butter

1 lb/455 g russet potatoes

2 cups/480 ml chicken or vegetable broth

2 cups/480 ml heavy/double cream

Salt and pepper

Discard the roots and dark green part of the leeks and halve lengthwise. Rinse thoroughly under running water and cut them into slices ½ in/12 mm thick. Put the butter and leeks in a large saucepan and cook over medium heat, stirring occasionally, for 8 to 10 minutes, or until the leeks are soft.

Meanwhile, peel the potatoes and dice them into cubes ½ in/ 12 mm thick. Add the potatoes and broth to the pan, bring it to a boil, and cook for 15 minutes, or until the potatoes are soft. Add the cream and simmer until warm. (Do not allow it to boil.) Season with salt and pepper and serve immediately.

On the Lighter Side

We made this soup the traditional way, using cream to thicken it and give it a smooth texture. Although there is nothing that compares to that silky texture, there are times when you don't want to invest all those calories. By making a few simple changes, you can cut the calories in half and reduce the fat by 45 g per serving, without losing any of the flavor.

Cook the leeks in 3 tbsp butter until soft, stir in 2 tbsp flour, and cook until bubbly. Slowly stir in 2 cups/480 ml of stock and the potatoes and cook until the potatoes are soft. Stir in 1 cup/240 ml skim milk and season with salt and pepper.

HOT AND SOUR SOUP

Jill

The first time I made hot and sour soup, I went to buy the dried shiitake mushrooms the recipe called for and discovered they were very expensive for a tiny package! I don't think so. I like hot and sour soup, but not that much. So I bought a package of oyster mushrooms that cost about half as much, and the soup still tasted great. More expensive isn't always better.

One ½-oz/15-g package dried oyster mushrooms

One 5-oz/140-g can bamboo shoots

4 oz/115 g firm tofu

2 green/spring onions

4 cups/960 ml chicken broth

2 tbsp rice wine vinegar

1½ tbsp soy sauce

1 tsp Asian chili paste

Salt and pepper

2 tbsp cornstarch/cornflour

1 egg

Slice the mushrooms into thin strips and soak them in 1 cup/ 240 ml warm water for 15 minutes, or until soft. Drain the bamboo shoots and halve them lengthwise. Cut the tofu into cubes ½ in/12 mm thick. Thinly slice the white and light green parts of the green/spring onions.

Put the broth, vinegar, soy sauce, and chili paste in a large saucepan and bring to a boil. Simmer over medium heat for 5 minutes. Season with salt and pepper. Add the mushrooms with the water, the bamboo shoots, and the tofu and simmer for 5 minutes.

Combine the cornstarch/cornflour and ¼ cup/60 ml warm water and add to the pan, stirring constantly. Simmer for 2 minutes, or until slightly thickened. Beat the egg well and, stirring slowly, pour it into the soup. Cook for 30 seconds, until the egg is cooked and whispy, add the green/spring onions, and remove from the heat. Serve immediately.

35

BLUE CHEESE, PEAR, AND WALNUT SALAD

Megan   I love everything about this salad! The tang of the blue cheese, the sweet crunch of the pears and walnuts, and the peppery crispness of the arugula/rocket create the perfect combination of flavors. It's a great salad to serve to friends, but I prefer to keep it all to myself. I prepare the walnuts and dressing ahead of time. That way I can just toss the rest of the ingredients together and take it for lunch as often as I want . . . which is very often.

¾ cup/85 g walnuts

2 tbsp sugar

2 tbsp honey

¼ cup/60 ml olive oil

2 tbsp balsamic vinegar

2 tsp brown mustard

Salt and pepper

1 cup/30 g arugula/rocket

6 oz/170 g mixed greens

½ small red onion

2 ripe Bosc or Bartlett/Williams pears

½ cup/55 g crumbled blue cheese

Preheat the oven to 325°F/165°C/gas mark 3.

Spread the walnuts on a baking sheet/tray and bake for 10 minutes, or until toasted.

Put the sugar and honey in a frying pan and cook over medium heat, stirring frequently, for 10 minutes, or until the sugar is melted. Add the nuts and stir until they are completely coated. Pour the nut mixture onto a parchment/baking paper–lined baking sheet/tray to cool. Coarsely chop the walnuts and set aside.

Put the olive oil, vinegar, mustard, and salt in a small bowl and stir with a fork until completely combined. Put the arugula/rocket and mixed greens in a serving bowl, pour in the vinaigrette, and toss until the greens are completely coated.

Thinly slice the onion and sprinkle it over the salad. Peel, halve, and core the pears. Thinly slice the pears and arrange them on the salad. Sprinkle the cheese and candied walnuts over the pears and serve immediately or refrigerate until ready to serve.

On a Budget

Nuts can be expensive, especially if you buy the small packages of chopped nuts. If you're lucky, you can get them in the bulk section of a store. If not, make sure to check the store labels for the cost per ounce. Usually the larger packages are substantially cheaper. Unused nuts can be put in an airtight container and frozen. They will last for years, and you will always have them when you need them.

SPINACH SALAD WITH WARM CITRUS VINAIGRETTE

Jill

Okay, so here's another one of those dishes that I had in a restaurant and had to re-create at home. The place that I always order this has a lunch special: all-you-can eat soup and salad for a bargain. Huge mistake on their part. I have no doubt they lose money on me. I'd be embarrassed to admit how many refills I can eat of this salad. But really, it can't be that bad to scarf down a ton of it—after all, it's salad. At least that's what I keep trying to convince myself.

1 red bell pepper/capsicum

½ cup/55 g sliced/flaked almonds

8 slices bacon/streaky bacon

1 orange

1 tbsp honey

⅓ cup/75 ml olive oil

Salt and pepper

6 oz/170 g baby spinach

¼ cup/30 g thinly sliced red onion

Place the bell pepper/capsicum directly on the burner of a gas stove or under the broiler of an electric stove. Cook for 10 minutes, holding with tongs and turning occasionally, until almost completely black on all sides. Put in a bowl, cover tightly with plastic wrap/cling film, and let it stand for 10 minutes to steam. Scrape the skin from the flesh, cut in half, and remove the seeds. Cut into strips ¼ in/6 mm wide.

Put the almonds in a dry frying pan and cook over medium heat, stirring occasionally, for 8 minutes, or until lightly browned. Remove the nuts from the pan and set aside.

Cut the bacon into strips ¼ in/6 mm wide and put them in the small frying pan. Cook over medium-high heat, stirring occasionally, for 10 minutes, or until crisp. Drain on paper towels/absorbent paper.

Grate 1 tsp of zest from the orange and put it in a small saucepan. Juice the orange and add ¼ cup/60 ml of the juice to the pan. Add the honey and olive oil and cook over medium heat for 5 minutes, or until warm. Season with salt and pepper.

Divide the spinach among four bowls and sprinkle some of the roasted pepper, almonds, bacon, and onion on each salad. Spoon the warm vinaigrette over the salads and serve immediately.

Cooking Tip

Juicing citrus falls under the category of "skip the fancy tools." Instead of buying a fancy juicer, cut the citrus in half and poke it a few times with a fork. Stick the fork in the fruit and twist it around as you squeeze the juice into a bowl. That's it.

SPINACH SOUFFLÉ

 Megan

Don't let the word *soufflé* scare you. This one doesn't fall easily. It's very stable (and very green). The first time I made this for my boyfriend, I set it on the table and he said, "Well, that looks . . . healthy." Not the best compliment ever, but I won him over in the end. It may look healthy, but it tastes delicious.

Grated Parmesan cheese for dusting

4 green/spring onions

¼ cup/55 g butter

¼ cup/30 g flour

1 cup/240 ml milk

1 tsp salt

½ tsp pepper

4 large eggs, separated

10 oz/280 g frozen spinach, thawed

1 cup/115 g shredded Cheddar or Jack cheese

Preheat the oven to 350°F/180°C/gas mark 4. Lightly butter or oil a 2 qt/2 L soufflé/baking dish and dust it with Parmesan cheese.

Finely chop the white and light green parts of the green/spring onions. Melt the butter in a large saucepan over medium heat and add the onions. Cook for 1 minute. Stir in the flour and cook, stirring constantly, for 1 minute, or until bubbly. Slowly stir or whisk in the milk and bring it to a boil. Add the salt and pepper and cook for 1 minute, or until thickened. Slowly whisk the egg yolks into the milk mixture. Add the spinach and cheese, mix well, and remove the pan from the heat.

Put the egg whites in a bowl and whip on high speed for 3 minutes, or until stiff peaks form. (When you lift the beaters out of the eggs, they should form peaks that stay upright.) Stir about one quarter of the egg whites into the spinach mixture to loosen it up. Add the remaining egg whites and, using a spatula, fold the egg whites into the spinach mixture by carefully sliding the spatula down one side of the pan, across the bottom, and pulling the spinach mixture up over the egg whites. Repeat the process until only a few streaks of egg white remain. Do not overmix, or the eggs will deflate. Pour the mixture into the prepared pan and bake for 35 to 40 minutes, or until the soufflé is golden brown and doesn't jiggle in the middle when you move the pan slightly. Serve immediately.

> ## Cooking Tip
>
> Egg whites will not get frothy if there is any fat in them, and egg yolks contain fat. Always separate the egg white into a small bowl first. Once it is separated, put the white in one bowl with the other whites and the yolks in a separate bowl. That way you can outwit the Murphy's Law corollary that states that when separating six eggs into the same bowl, you will break only the last yolk.

TWO-POTATO GRATIN

Jill

There is nothing better on a cold winter day than a bubbling-hot potato gratin. You can serve it as a main dish with a crisp salad or as a side dish with roasted chicken or beef. It's better if you steer clear of the skim milk on this one and use 2 percent or whole milk in order to give it the right consistency. And don't miss the variation: The combination of sweet potatoes and apples is the perfect accompaniment to roasted pork.

1 clove garlic

1 lb/455 g russet potatoes (2 or 3)

1 lb/455 g red potatoes (4 or 5)

2 cups/480 ml milk

1½ tsp salt

1 tsp dried thyme

Preheat the oven to 375°F/190°C/gas mark 5.

Cut the garlic in half and rub over the sides and bottom of a 10-in/25-cm shallow baking dish.

Peel and thinly slice all of the potatoes. Put the potatoes, milk, salt, and thyme in a large saucepan and bring to a simmer. Cook over medium-low heat for 8 minutes, or until the potatoes just begin to get tender, stirring frequently to keep the potatoes from sticking to the bottom of the pan.

Pour the potato-milk mixture into the prepared baking dish and press them into a flat layer. Bake for 35 to 40 minutes, or until golden brown. Let stand for 5 minutes before serving.

variation SWEET POTATO, APPLE, AND LEEK GRATIN

Use 1½ lb/680 g thinly sliced sweet potatoes, 2 cups/480 ml milk, 1 chopped leek, 3 peeled and thinly sliced apples, 2 tbsp flour, 1 tbsp grated peeled fresh ginger, 1 tsp curry powder, and ½ tsp ground cinnamon. Combine the flour, ginger, curry powder, and cinnamon in a small bowl. Place one third of the sweet potatoes in a layer in the bottom of a 10-in/25-cm baking dish, top with half of the apples and leeks, and sprinkle with half of the flour mixture. Repeat to form an additional layer and top with the remaining sweet potatoes. Pour the milk over, and bake as directed.

Chapter

2

PASTA

Pasta dishes are some of the simplest to prepare and the easiest to adjust to your own tastes. They are excellent with any type of meat, seafood, or vegetable. But, no matter what amazing combination of ingredients you come up with, the key to a great pasta dish is still perfectly cooked pasta. The good news is that's very easy to achieve by using plenty of boiling salted water, stirring occasionally, and cooking until it's just al dente. As basic as those three things may seem, they're all very important. Use the largest saucepan you have. Too much water doesn't matter, while not enough water will leave you with a starchy, gelatinous lump. Make sure the water is at a rolling boil before adding the pasta. If the water isn't boiling, the pasta will cook too slowly and become a starchy, gelatinous lump. (Are you seeing a trend here?) And, don't forget the salt! Pasta needs salt to bring out the flavor. Make sure to stir the pasta occasionally while it's cooking. We've all forgotten before. You put the pasta in the pan, stir it, and get busy doing something else. Ten minutes later, you go back and the pasta is all stuck together in—you guessed it—a starchy, gelatinous lump. Check the pasta frequently toward the end of the cooking time. It should be al dente, which literally means "to the tooth." It should offer slight resistance when you bite into it but not be chewy.

There are many different kinds of pasta. In fact, the National Pasta Association lists more than fifty shapes on their Web site. Don't panic—you don't need to know them all. Just follow the basic rule that light, thin pastas go with light, delicate sauces and heavy, thick pastas go with heavy, chunky sauces. It's really about balance; the pasta and the sauce should have equal billing. If you make a dish and the sauce is great, but the pasta gets lost, try a heavier pasta next time and vice versa.

There are four basic sauces that we use repeatedly with pasta: Marinara Sauce (facing page), Garlic and Oil Sauce (facing page), Alfredo Sauce (page 44), Pesto Sauce (page 44). Each of these has a very different and distinct flavor. They are all simple to prepare and all lend themselves well to the addition of different meats or vegetables.

MARINARA SAUCE

MAKES ABOUT 6 CUPS/1.4 L

This is a basic marinara sauce that is quick to prepare and can be used a million different ways. We usually make a double batch because it doesn't take any longer and we can freeze the extra to use later. We added sugar to offset the acidity of the tomatoes. We know this isn't the traditional Italian method, but we're not Italian, and we like it better this way. If you're a purist, leave the sugar out.

1 onion

2 carrots

2 stalks celery

2 cloves garlic

¼ cup/60 ml olive oil

Two 28-oz/795-g cans crushed tomatoes, juices reserved

¼ cup/50 g sugar

1 tsp dried Italian seasoning

Salt and pepper

Peel the onion and carrots and cut them into pieces ¼ in/6 mm thick. Cut the celery into pieces ¼ in/6 mm thick. Peel and finely chop the garlic.

Put the olive oil in a large saucepan over medium-high heat. Add the onion, celery, and carrots and cook, stirring frequently, for 10 minutes, or until the vegetables are soft. Add the garlic and cook for 1 minute. Add the tomatoes with the juice, sugar, and Italian seasoning, and season with salt and pepper. Bring to a boil, reduce to low heat, and simmer for 30 minutes, until the tomatoes break down and become saucy. Remove from the heat and adjust the seasoning. The sauce can be used immediately, refrigerated for several days, or frozen for several months.

43

GARLIC AND OIL SAUCE

MAKES ENOUGH TO COAT 1 LB/445 G COOKED PASTA

We included this recipe so you could see the basic proportions, but there is no need to make this sauce separately. You can make it right in the pasta pan while the pasta is draining and save yourself an extra dish to wash.

5 cloves garlic

⅓ cup/75 ml olive oil

¼ cup/10 g chopped fresh parsley

Peel and finely chop the garlic. Put the olive oil and garlic in a saucepan and cook over medium-low heat for 10 minutes, or until the garlic just begins to turn pale gold. Stir in the parsley and use immediately.

ALFREDO SAUCE

The key to perfectly smooth Alfredo sauce is freshly grated Parmesan cheese. The canned stuff just doesn't melt as well. In our recipes, we make the sauce in the pan with the pasta, but it can be a little more difficult to get it smooth. The first few times you try it, you may want to make the sauce separately or remove all of the other ingredients from the pan.

1 clove garlic

2 tbsp butter

½ cup/120 ml heavy/double cream

¾ cup/85 g freshly grated Parmesan cheese

Peel and finely chop the garlic. Put the butter and cream in a small saucepan and cook over medium heat for 5 minutes, or until the butter is melted. Add the cheese and garlic and stir until smooth. The sauce can be used immediately or refrigerated for several days.

PESTO SAUCE

We love pesto so much that we got a couple of basil plants to put on our balcony so we always have it handy. If you're buying the little 2-ounce bags of pine nuts, make a double batch of this recipe so you can use the whole bag. Pine nuts don't have a very long shelf life, and those little bags get lost in the cabinet. You can freeze the extra sauce in one-half cup portions so later you can just grab the amount you need. This pesto sauce also tastes just as great made with walnuts, which are substantially cheaper.

One ⅔-oz/20-g package fresh basil

4 cloves garlic

½ cup/120 ml olive oil

¼ cup/30 g freshly grated Parmesan cheese

3 tbsp pine nuts or chopped walnuts

Stem the basil. Peel the garlic. Put the basil leaves, garlic, olive oil, cheese, and nuts in a blender and pulse until smooth. Cover tightly and refrigerate for up to 1 week or freeze for several months.

PASTA SALAD WITH SMOKED SALMON, ASPARAGUS, AND LEMON VINAIGRETTE

Megan

I use cold-smoked salmon (see below) for this dish because the delicate smokiness and the soft texture go well with the asparagus and vinaigrette. You can use hot smoked salmon instead; just make sure its flavoring doesn't overpower the vinaigrette. Anything with citrus or herb flavors would be fine, but stay away from strong or specific flavors like teriyaki or maple.

12 oz/340 g dry rotini or bowtie pasta

1 lb/455 g asparagus

4 oz/115 g cold-smoked salmon

1 cup/140 g grape tomatoes

1 large shallot

1 lemon

⅓ cup/75 ml olive oil

Salt and pepper

Bring a large saucepan of salted water to a boil. Add the pasta and cook, stirring occasionally, for 10 minutes, or until al dente. Drain the pasta, rinse it under cold running water, and put it in a large bowl.

Meanwhile, break the ends off of the asparagus and cut the spears into pieces 1 in/2.5 cm long. Put the asparagus in a microwave-safe bowl and add enough water to just cover the bottom of the bowl. Cover tightly with plastic wrap/cling film and microwave on high for 4 minutes, or until tender-crisp. Carefully uncover, drain, and let cool.

Cut the salmon into strips ¼ by 1 in/6 mm by 2.5 cm. Cut any large grape tomatoes in half. Finely chop the shallot. Add the salmon, tomatoes, and shallot to the bowl of pasta.

Grate 1 tsp of the zest from the lemon and put it in a small bowl. Juice the lemon and add the juice to the bowl along with the olive oil. Stir well and add to the pasta. Season with salt and pepper and stir until combined. Refrigerate until ready to serve.

Ingredient Info

Salmon can be purchased four ways: fresh, cured, cold smoked, and hot smoked. Fresh salmon is, well, just fresh. Cured salmon is coated with a mixture of salt, sugar, and spices or flavorings and then refrigerated for several days before packaging. Cured salmon is usually marketed under the name "gravlax" or just "lox." Cold-smoked salmon is generally cured for 24 to 48 hours and then smoked in a special room that allows the smoke in, but no heat. It gets a delicate smoky flavor, but the salmon is not cooked so the flesh remains translucent. Hot-smoked salmon is usually coated with herbs or flavorings and then smoked over heat. It develops a stronger smoky flavor, and the fish gets completely cooked through. The different varieties are all delicious; you just have to decide which flavor and consistency works best in your dish.

SPICY SOBA NOODLES

Megan

This dish was voted the worst-looking, but best-tasting dish one night by our ace team of taste-testers. Despite their strange color, soba noodles are tasty and good for you. They are made with buckwheat—a grain that was originally cultivated in Asia. They contain no gluten but have lots of minerals like iron and magnesium. This is also really good with smoked tofu or shrimp/prawns.

¹⁄₃ cup/75 ml soy sauce

1 tbsp Asian chili paste

1 tbsp brown sugar

3 cloves garlic

8 oz/225 g fresh cremini/brown mushrooms

4 green/spring onions

1 head bok choy

3 tbsp sesame seeds

2 tbsp canola oil

2 tbsp finely chopped peeled fresh ginger

10 oz/280 g dry soba noodles

1 cup/155 g frozen shelled edamame

Combine ¹⁄₃ cup/75 ml water with the soy sauce, chili paste, and brown sugar in a small bowl and set aside.

Peel and finely chop the garlic. Remove the stem ends from the mushrooms and thinly slice the caps. Thinly slice the white and light green parts of the green/spring onions. Thinly slice the bok choy crosswise.

Put the sesame seeds in a large, dry frying pan and toast them over medium heat, stirring frequently, for 5 minutes, or until lightly browned. Remove the sesame seeds from the pan and set aside.

Put the canola oil in the frying pan over medium-high heat. Add the ginger and garlic and cook, stirring constantly, for 30 seconds. Add the mushrooms and cook, stirring frequently, for 6 minutes, or until they start to brown. Lower the heat to medium, add the bok choy and green/spring onions, and cook for 5 minutes, or until the bok choy is still tender-crisp. Add the soy sauce mixture and cook, stirring frequently, for 2 minutes, or until the sauce is hot.

Meanwhile, bring a saucepan of salted water to a boil. Add the noodles and edamame and cook for 6 minutes, stirring occasionally, or until the noodles are al dente. Drain the noodles and edamame and put them in a large bowl. Add the vegetable mixture and sesame seeds and toss until combined. Serve immediately.

LEFTOVER RAVIOLI

These ravioli are a great way to use up leftovers without anyone noticing. You can use just about anything in them. I've used chicken, beef, pork, broccoli, cauliflower, squash/courgette, ricotta, mozzarella, and Parmesan in myriad combinations. Once I even used leftover chicken pot pie filling. It tasted good, but I'll admit it was a little weird to see the whole peas in there. The point is, use what you have in a combination that sounds good to you. If the idea of coming up with your own combination makes you nervous, stick with meat and cheese or a blend of cheeses, and you can't go wrong.

Forty small 3-in/7-cm wonton wrappers

1¼ cups/300 ml finely chopped leftover meat and/or vegetables

1 cup/240 ml Pesto Sauce (page 44)

Bring a large saucepan of salted water to a boil.

Lay out twenty wonton wrappers and place 1 tbsp of your chosen filling on each one. Using a pastry brush or your finger, wet the edges of one of the wonton skins. Top with another wonton skin and press firmly around three edges. Press lightly on the center of the ravioli to remove any air and seal the last edge. Repeat with the remaining wrappers.

Put the ravioli in the boiling water (put them all in at the same time if they can fit into your pot without crowding) and cook for 3 minutes. To test their doneness, scoop out one ravioli and slice off a corner. If the wrapper is tender yet a bit toothsome, they are done. If not, cook for 1 minute more, retest, and repeat until cooked through. Drain the ravioli and return them to the pot. Add the pesto and cook over medium heat for 1 minute, or until warm. Serve immediately.

> ### Cooking Tip
>
> Pressing the air out of the ravioli before you seal it may not seem necessary, but air expands as it heats. That means that too much air in the ravioli will cause them to pop open and all of your filling will be floating in the water instead of staying inside the ravioli.

SHRIMP ALFREDO WITH SNAP PEAS AND PASTA

Jill

I used penne or bowtie pasta here because they have crevices that grab the sauce and they are equal in size to the other ingredients. If you'd rather use strand pasta, stick with heavier versions like linguine or fettuccine. You can use any size shrimp/prawns for this dish. If I'm making this for myself, I use whatever's cheapest. If I'm making it for friends, I usually use large (21–30 count) or extra-large (16–20 count) shellfish.

12 oz/340 g dry penne or bowtie pasta

1 lb/455 g raw shrimp/prawns

1 tbsp olive oil

1½ cups/100 g snap peas

1 small clove garlic

2 tbsp butter

½ cup/120 ml heavy/double cream

¾ cup/85 g freshly grated Parmesan cheese

Salt and pepper

1 tbsp chopped fresh parsley

Bring a large saucepan of salted water to a boil. Add the pasta and cook, stirring occasionally, for 10 minutes, or until al dente. Drain the pasta and keep warm.

Meanwhile, peel the shrimp/prawns. Heat the olive oil in a large frying pan over medium-high heat. Add the snap peas and cook, stirring frequently, for 3 minutes. Add the shellfish and cook, stirring frequently for 2 minutes, or until they are light pink and start to curl up. Remove the contents from the pan and set aside.

Peel and finely chop the garlic. Put the butter and cream in the pan and cook over medium heat for 5 minutes, or until the butter is melted. Add the cheese and garlic and stir until smooth. Season with salt and pepper. Stir the shrimp/prawns and snap peas into the sauce and add the pasta. Stir until the pasta is completely coated with the sauce. Remove from the heat, sprinkle with the parsley, and serve immediately.

49

·variation· SHRIMP DIJON

Substitute 8 oz/225 g quartered fresh mushrooms for the snap peas and cook for an additional 5 minutes. Stir 3 tbsp Dijon mustard into the sauce once it is smooth.

BRUSCHETTA PASTA

Jill

I had something similar to this in a restaurant once. It was good, but of course I think this version is way better, mostly because I get to put in as much garlic and basil as I want—which means it has to be delicious. I may not be nice to talk to afterward, but at least I know I am vampire-safe.

1 lb/455 g boneless, skinless chicken breasts (2 or 3)

Salt and pepper

12 oz/340 g dry angel hair pasta

4 large tomatoes

4 cloves garlic

One ²/₃-oz/20-g package fresh basil

2 tbsp olive oil

1 tbsp balsamic vinegar

¼ cup/30 g freshly grated Parmesan cheese

Preheat a grill/barbecue or grill pan on high heat.

Season the chicken with salt and pepper and put it on the grill/barbecue. Cook for 5 minutes on each side, or until cooked through. Let stand tor 5 minutes and then cut each chicken breast into slices ¼ in/6 mm thick. Keep warm.

Bring a large saucepan of salted water to a boil. Add the pasta and cook, stirring occasionally, for 6 minutes, or until al dente. Drain the pasta and keep warm.

Meanwhile, halve, seed, and cut the tomatoes into pieces ¼ in/6 mm wide. Peel and finely chop the garlic. Remove the basil stems and roughly chop the leaves. Combine the tomatoes, basil, garlic, and olive oil in a bowl and season with salt and pepper.

Divide the chicken among four plates and top with some of the pasta. Scatter the tomato mixture over the pasta. Drizzle the vinegar over the tomatoes and sprinkle with the Parmesan. Serve immediately.

51

On the Lighter Side

It drives me crazy when people talk about pasta being fattening. This dish is about 525 calories per serving exactly as it is written. That includes about 1½ cups/360 ml of pasta per serving, which is a big portion. If that seems like too many calories for you, knock down the pasta to 1 cup. You'll save about 100 calories, and it's still a good-size portion. So, you can have delicious, satisfying pasta loaded with fresh flavors or a frozen diet meal with six pieces of limp pasta, some soggy vegetables, and a couple pieces of chicken. Not much thought needed on that one.

CHICKEN LINGUINI IN GARLIC SAUCE

Jill I love garlic! And this recipe allows me to indulge myself. Garlic sauces are nice because they're light, have a lot of flavor, and literally go with anything. This is a great solution for when you're thinking "Oh, man, I have to use up that (fill in the blank) before it goes bad,"—because everything tastes better with a little garlic!

12 oz/340 g dry linguini

1 lb/455 g boneless, skinless chicken breasts (2 or 3)

1 red bell pepper/capsicum

1 lb/455 g fresh mushrooms

5 cloves garlic

¼ cup/60 ml olive oil

1 tsp fresh lemon zest

Salt and pepper

Bring a large saucepan of salted water to a boil. Add the pasta and cook, stirring occasionally, for 10 minutes, or until al dente. Drain the pasta and keep warm.

Cut the chicken into thin strips. Halve, seed, and cut the bell pepper/capsicum into pieces ½ in/12 mm wide. Remove the stem ends of the mushrooms and cut the caps in half. Peel and finely chop the garlic.

Put 1 tbsp of the olive oil in a large frying pan over medium-high heat. Add the mushrooms and peppers/capsicums and cook, stirring frequently, for 10 minutes, or until browned. Push the mushroom mixture to the sides of the pan and add the chicken. Cook, stirring frequently, for 5 minutes, or until the chicken is cooked through. Add the garlic and cook, stirring constantly, for 1 minute. Add the pasta, lemon zest, and the remaining 3 tbsp oil. Season with salt and pepper and toss until evenly coated. Serve immediately.

On a Budget

I love red bell peppers/capsicums and use them a lot. Unfortunately, it always seems that they aren't on sale when I need them. I have started buying a dozen when they are on sale. I slice a few, dice some, and roast the rest. Then I put them on a baking sheet/tray in the freezer. Once they are frozen, I put them in resealable bags. Freezing softens the raw ones a little, but they still work great if you are cooking them. The roasted peppers are perfect simply thawed out.

PENNE BURINA

Megan

I cannot, in good faith, take credit for this delicious, spicy dish. If I tried, I would never be forgiven by the "copyright police," a.k.a. my boyfriend, Michi. This is one of his favorite pasta dishes and was the first thing he ever cooked for me (imagine candlelight and "O Sole Mio" playing in the background). Needless to say, I was hooked. It has become one of our standard dishes, and it goes well with any of those fifty types of pasta recognized by the National Pasta Association!

12 oz/340 g dry penne pasta

8 oz/225 g bacon/streaky bacon

1 large onion

8 oz/225 g fresh mushrooms

2 cloves garlic

1 tsp cayenne pepper

½ tsp dry Italian seasoning

Two 15-oz/430-g cans diced tomatoes

2 tbsp cornstarch/cornflour

½ cup/120 ml milk

Salt and pepper

1 cup/120 g frozen peas

Grated Parmesan cheese

Bring a large saucepan of salted water to a boil. Add the pasta and cook, stirring occasionally, for 10 minutes, or until al dente. Drain the pasta and keep warm.

Cut the bacon into strips ½ in/12 mm wide. Peel the onion and chop it into pieces ½ in/12 mm wide. Remove the stem ends from the mushrooms and slice the caps. Peel and finely chop the garlic.

Put the bacon in a large frying pan and cook over medium heat, stirring occasionally, for 8 minutes, or until the bacon just begins to get crisp. Drain the bacon grease from the pan and add the onion and mushrooms. Cook, stirring occasionally, for 10 minutes, or until the onion is soft. Stir in the garlic, cayenne, and Italian seasoning and cook for 1 minute. Add the tomatoes and bring to a simmer. Whisk together the cornstarch/cornflour and milk and stir them into the tomato sauce. Season with salt and pepper and add the peas. Simmer, stirring frequently, for 3 minutes, or until the peas are hot.

Divide the pasta among four bowls, top with some of the sauce, and sprinkle with Parmesan cheese to serve.

53

Ingredient Info

This may seem pretty basic, but it has caused problems for a friend or two. When you buy fresh garlic, it comes in a bulb or head. The small sections that break off are the cloves. Don't confuse the two. If you use two bulbs of garlic instead of two cloves, not only will your food be inedible, but it will take weeks to get the smell out of your house.

CAJUN PASTA

This recipe is a delicious way to spice up your pasta repertoire. With a combination of the standard Cajun ingredients—onions, celery, and lots of andouille sausage—your taste buds won't know what hit them. You could substitute shrimp/prawns for the chicken for a little fancier (but more expensive) version.

12 oz/340 g dry penne pasta

12 oz/340 g andouille sausage

8 oz/225 g boneless, skinless chicken breasts (1 or 2)

2 cloves garlic

1 small yellow onion

1 stalk celery

1 green bell pepper/capsicum

3 green/spring onions

1 tbsp dry Cajun seasoning

2 tbsp flour

1 cup/240 ml chicken broth

One 15-oz/430-g can diced tomatoes

Salt and pepper

Bring a large saucepan of salted water to a boil. Cook the pasta, stirring occasionally, for 10 minutes, or until al dente. Drain and keep warm.

Cut the sausage into slices ¼ in/6 mm thick. Cut the chicken into pieces 1 in/12 mm wide. Peel and finely chop the garlic. Peel the onion and chop it into pieces ¼ in/6 mm long. Cut the celery into pieces ¼ in/6 mm long. Halve, stem, and seed the green bell pepper/capsicum and cut it into pieces ¼ in/6 mm long. Thinly slice the white and light green parts of the green/spring onions.

Put the sausage in a large frying pan and cook over medium heat for 5 minutes, or until there is some fat from the sausage in the pan. Add the chicken and cook, stirring frequently, for 5 minutes, or until the chicken is cooked on the outside. Add the garlic, bell pepper/capsicum, celery, and yellow onion and cook for 10 minutes, or until the vegetables are soft. Add the Cajun seasoning and flour to the pan and cook, stirring constantly, for 2 minutes. Slowly add the broth, stirring until the sauce is smooth. Add the tomatoes, season with salt and pepper, and simmer for 10 minutes for the flavors to meld. Add the pasta and green/spring onions to the pan and stir until combined. Serve immediately.

55

Lingo

Here are a couple of terms you may have heard: **Mirepoix** (meer-PWAH) and the **Trinity.** Mirepoix has its roots in French cooking and the Trinity comes from Cajun cooking, but both have recently become more mainstream terms. Mirepoix is a combination of chopped onion, celery, and carrot, usually made with 50 percent onion and 25 percent each celery and carrot. The trinity consists of onion, celery, and green bell pepper, usually in equal parts. They are used as the first layer of flavor for many sauces, soups, and stews.

SPAGHETTI WITH CHICKEN MEATBALLS

Megan

There is nothing more satisfying than a big plate of spaghetti and meatballs, but there is no denying what a few too many meatballs can do to your waistline. I decided to try making the meatballs with ground/minced chicken (use chicken thigh instead of ground breast for moister meatballs) instead of beef, and they are just as delicious yet cut the calories in half. If you are more of a traditionalist, simply substitute beef for all or half of the chicken.

½ small onion

2 cloves garlic

1 lb/455 g ground/minced chicken

½ cup/55 g dry bread crumbs

1 egg

½ tsp dry Italian seasoning

½ tsp salt

1 tbsp olive oil

4 cups/1 L Marinara Sauce (page 43)

12 oz/340 g dry spaghetti

Grated Parmesan cheese

Peel and finely chop the onion and garlic and put them in a large bowl. Add the chicken, bread crumbs, egg, Italian seasoning, and salt. Stir until completely combined. Roll the mixture into balls 1 in/2.5 cm in diameter.

Pour the olive oil into a frying pan over medium-high heat. Add some of the meatballs and cook for 5 minutes, or until browned on all sides. Repeat until all of the meatballs are browned.

Meanwhile, put the marinara sauce and ½ cup/120 ml water in a large saucepan and bring to a boil. Add the meatballs to the sauce and simmer over medium-low heat for 30 minutes, until cooked through.

Bring a large saucepan of salted water to a boil. Add the pasta and cook, stirring occasionally, for 10 minutes, or until al dente. Drain the pasta and divide it among four pasta bowls. Top with the meatballs and sauce, sprinkle with the Parmesan, and serve immediately.

56

KEVIN'S TORTELLINI

Jill   This recipe is a nod to our former roommate Kevin, who made this for Megan and me. His original version involved lots of jars and boxes. We decided that this should involve some semblance of real food, so we made a lot of adjustments. Of course, we had him try the final version since the original creation was his. He approves.

1 lb/455 g Italian sausage

1 clove garlic

2 tbsp butter

½ cup/120 ml heavy/double cream

¾ cup/85 g freshly grated
Parmesan cheese

1 cup/240 ml Marinara Sauce
(page 43)

1 lb/455 g frozen cheese tortellini

1 cup/115 g shredded mozzarella
cheese

Preheat the oven to 350°F/180°C /gas mark 4.

Put the sausage in a large frying pan and break it into small pieces with a spoon. (If you bought sausage in the casing, squeeze it out of the casing.) Cook over medium-high heat for 10 minutes, or until cooked through.

Peel and finely chop the garlic. Put the butter and cream in a small saucepan and cook over medium heat for 5 minutes, or until the butter is melted. Add the Parmesan and garlic and stir until smooth. Remove from the heat and stir in the marinara sauce.

Put the frozen tortellini in an 8-in/20-cm square baking dish, add the sausage and marinara mixture, and stir until completely combined. Sprinkle with the mozzarella and bake for 30 minutes, or until the cheese is lightly browned. Serve immediately.

On a Budget

Italian sausage is usually more expensive than ground/minced pork. When you are using loose sausage, as for the tortellini or lasagna, it's simple to make your own. Just combine 1 lb/455 g ground pork with 1 tbsp finely chopped red bell pepper/capsicum, 1 tbsp fennel seeds, 1 tsp finely chopped garlic, 1 tsp black pepper, and ¼ tsp red pepper flakes, and you have Italian sausage.

BAKED ZITI

Megan

I make this dish with ziti pasta, but you can use penne or mostaccioli instead. They are all similar in size and shape. I think I use ziti because it sounds better. Baked ziti or baked penne sound more interesting. Baked mostaccioli sounds like old-people food . . . sorry, Mom!

1 lb/455 g dry ziti pasta

One ²/₃-oz/20-g package fresh basil

4 cups/960 ml Marinara Sauce
(page 43)

2 cups/230 g shredded mozzarella
cheese

Preheat the oven to 350°F/180°C/gas mark 4. Lightly oil, or coat with cooking spray, a 9-in/23-cm square baking dish or a 2-qt/2-L baking dish.

Bring a large saucepan of salted water to a boil. Add the ziti and cook, stirring occasionally, for 12 minutes, or until al dente. Drain the pasta and put it in the prepared dish.

Roughly chop the basil leaves and put them in the pan. Pour the sauce on top, sprinkle 1 cup/115 g of the cheese over the pasta, and stir until combined. Top with the remaining 1 cup/115 g of cheese and bake for 30 minutes, or until the cheese is lightly browned. Serve immediately.

59

Cooking Tip

The easiest way to cut leafy vegetables is to stack the leaves and roll them up like a cigar. This is called a "chiffonade." You can cut them in thin strips for garnish or just continue chopping from there. It allows you to cut more at once and be precise for thin strips. It also gives you more to hang on to and keeps them from flying all over.

LASAGNA

Jill

Lasagna is amazing. It's basically a mechanism to eat massive quantities of meat and cheese, which means that it has to be delicious. If meat isn't your thing, you can easily substitute vegetables, tofu, or textured vegetable protein. Or put in more cheese! You can never go wrong with more cheese. The nice part about this version is you don't even have to boil the noodles. You just put it together and leave it in the fridge for a few hours. That's my speed.

1 lb/455 g ground/minced beef

1 lb/455 g bulk Italian sausage

7 cups/1.7 L Marinara Sauce (page 43)

1 lb/455 g dry lasagna noodles

2 lb/910 g cottage cheese or ricotta cheese

4 cups/455 g shredded mozzarella cheese

Crumble the beef and sausage into a large frying pan and cook over medium heat, breaking apart any large pieces, for 10 minutes, or until cooked through. Drain off the fat and stir in the marinara sauce.

Spoon a little of the sauce into a 9-by-13-in/23-by-32-cm baking dish and spread it around to cover the bottom. (This is just to keep the pasta from sticking to the bottom of the dish.) Arrange a layer of uncooked noodles over the sauce and top with one third of the remaining sauce. Spread one half of the cottage cheese over the sauce and top with one third of the mozzarella. Add another layer of noodles, sauce, cottage cheese, and mozzarella. Add a final layer of noodles, sauce, and mozzarella cheese. Cover the pan with aluminum foil coated with cooking spray and refrigerate for at least 4 hours or overnight.

Preheat the oven to 350°F/180°C/gas mark 4.

Bake the lasagna for 1 hour or until heated through (insert a knife blade in the center, remove, and then touch the blade to test how hot the lasagna is in the center). Remove the aluminum foil and bake for 30 minutes, or until the cheese is lightly browned. Serve immediately.

On a Budget

Cheese can be expensive, but it often goes on sale. We have a store in our area that puts 8-oz/25-g bags of shredded cheese on sale several times a year. When that happens, we stock up and keep it in the freezer until we're ready to use it.

Chapter 3

SEAFOOD

Buying fresh fish can be daunting even for the most experienced cooks. And if you're a first timer, all the fish and lobsters staring back at you can be scary, if not mildly creepy. You know that freshness is key—but where do you go from there? The most important indicator of freshness is smell. Fish should have a clean, fresh aroma reminiscent of the sea. If it smells fishy, it's on its way out. Whole fish should have moist, shiny skin. Dull or slimy skin indicates age. Fish fillets should be firm and spring back when gently pressed. If you leave finger marks when you press it, leave the fish in the store. You will be much happier substituting another type of fish.

Knowing which fish are fresh and worth buying is only half the battle. You also have to decide which type of fish will work best for the dish. This is especially important with fish since many times the choices are limited. We don't profess to be experts on fish, especially since we live in a desert, but we group them more by texture than by flavor. Since the fish is usually the main part of the dish, a little difference in flavor isn't going to matter. To us, the texture and how well it holds together after being cooked are bigger issues.

Flounder, trout, fluke, halibut, and **sole** are all flaky, delicate fish that will fall apart if they are handled too much after cooking. These are best cooked as whole fillets that simply need to be moved from the pan to the plate.

Tilapia, perch, catfish, cod, whitefish, walleye, and **haddock** are flaky, but they are a little sturdier and hold up to a little more handling. They can be stewed in a dish like the Mediterranean Cod with Rice (page 79) or made into Oven-Baked Fish and Chips (page 78) and will not disintegrate.

Salmon, tuna, mahi mahi, swordfish, grouper, monkfish, mackerel, snapper, and **sea bass** have a firm texture. These are often sold as steaks, and there's a reason for that. They handle much like meat. They are perfect for dishes like the Teriyaki Salmon with Jasmine

Rice (page 82), for which they get turned over during cooking. Tossing this kind of fish in the air with a double twisting somer-sault may break it apart, but that's about what it takes.

Unless you are buying straight off the dock, shrimp/prawns are always frozen. Don't be fooled by signs that say "fresh"; if you look at the fine print, it says "freshly thawed." If you're using it that day, buy it thawed, otherwise frozen is a better choice. Vendors have different names for the sizes; one company's large may be another's jumbo. Just pay attention to the numbers listed with the names. Prawns are sized by how many are in 1 lb/455 g. Those numbers are regulated and will be the same no matter who packages them. They range from U10 (under 10 per 1 lb/455 g) to 61–70. We generally use 41/50s or 36/40s for cooking and 31/35s or 26/30s for serving cold.

Mussels, oysters, and clams should be firmly closed and odorless. Use them within 24 hours of purchasing and throw away any shells that do not open during cooking.

FLAKY/
DELICATE

FLOUNDER
TROUT
FLUKE
HALIBUT
SOLE

TILAPIA
PERCH
CATFISH
COD
WHITEFISH
WALLEYE
HADDOCK

FLAKY/
STURDY

SALMON
TUNA
MAHI MAHI
SWORDFISH
GROUPER
MONKFISH
MACKEREL
SNAPPER
SEA BASS

FIRM

Back in the nineteenth century, a French chef developed the classification of the five "mother sauces." He determined that every other sauce was a variation of one of those five sauces. A sixth sauce was later added to this list. You've probably made several of these sauces without even knowing it.

Béchamel (BEH shah mehl) is a pale white sauce made with a light roux of flour and fat and milk. We used variations of this in the Ham and Gouda Crêpes with Garlic Cream Sauce (page 148) and in the Clam Chowder (page 71).

Espagnole (ehs pahn YOHL) is made with a dark roux and meat stock. The sauce for the Shrimp Étouffée (page 72) and the Cajun Pasta (page 55) are versions of this sauce.

Velouté (veh LOO tay) is made with a light roux and chicken stock. We used a version of this for the Chicken Curry (page 107).

Emulsions include hollandaise, which is a light sauce made by emulsifying egg yolks, butter, and lemon juice; and mayonnaise, which is emulsified egg yolks and oil.

Vinaigrettes are any combination of oil and vinegar or other acid.

Tomato is considered a mother sauce, although it was added later. This is what we think of as marinara sauce, and it is, obviously, very commonly used.

CRAB AND CORN CAKES

Jill

I absolutely love crab cakes, but I don't make them often because lump crab is not cheap. Adding corn helps stretch the crab and makes the cost a little more reasonable. This makes eight good-sized crab cakes, which is plenty for a meal for four or an appetizer for eight. Or you can really impress your friends and make about thirty small crab cakes to serve at a party. I guarantee they will disappear in seconds.

2 red bell peppers/capsicums

2 large eggs

1 jalapeño pepper

3 green/spring onions

8 oz/225 g fresh lump crab meat or two 6-oz/170-g cans

1 cup/255 g corn kernels

1 cup/115 g dry bread crumbs

2 tbsp fresh lime juice

Salt and pepper

¼ cup/60 ml mayonnaise

¼ cup/60 ml sour cream

½ tsp cayenne pepper

2 tbsp canola oil

Place the red bell peppers/capsicums directly on the burner of a gas stove or under the broiler of an electric stove. Cook for 10 minutes, turning occasionally with tongs, until almost completely black on all sides. Put in a bowl, cover tightly with plastic wrap/cling film, and let stand for 10 minutes to steam. Scrape the skin from the flesh, cut them in half, and remove the seeds. Cut half of one of the roasted peppers into pieces ¼ in/6 mm wide and put the pieces in a large bowl. Set aside the remaining roasted pepper.

Add the eggs to the bowl and beat well. Halve, seed, and finely chop the jalapeño. Thinly slice the white and light green parts of the green/spring onions. Add the onions, jalapeño, crab meat, corn, bread crumbs, and lime juice to the bowl and season with salt and pepper. Stir until combined. Form the crab mixture into eight patties, cover, and refrigerate for at least 15 minutes, or up to 8 hours.

Put the remaining roasted pepper, the mayonnaise, sour cream, and cayenne in a blender and puree until smooth. Season with salt and refrigerate until ready to use.

Heat the canola oil in a large frying pan and add the crab cakes if your pan is large enough to accommodate them all without crowding (if it isn't, cook four at a time in two batches). Cook for 5 minutes on each side, or until golden brown. Spoon some of the sauce on each plate and top with two crab cakes. Serve immediately.

69

Ingredient Info

A little caution is necessary when you're working with jalapeños. The juice can get on your hands, and if you touch your eyes or nose it makes them burn like crazy. The best solution is to use plastic gloves while cutting them and throw away the gloves when you are finished. But if you don't have gloves handy, just make sure to wash your hands several times with lots of soap and water when you are finished.

CIOPPINO

Jill

This is not a cheap dish to make, but it's delicious and always impressive, so I make it anyway (at least for my good friends). You can help the budget a little by adjusting the seafood you use. In our area, mussels are about half the price of clams, so I often double the mussels and skip the clams. You can also use salmon and cod and leave out one of the shellfish. Just make sure you have at least four different types of seafood. If you're serving this to guests, make the sauce ahead of time and then just bring it back to a boil and add the seafood when you are ready to eat. Serve this with a loaf of crusty bread to soak up the sauce.

One 28-oz/800-g can whole tomatoes

1 small onion

5 cloves garlic

8 fresh mussels

12 oz/340 g salmon or cod

2 tbsp olive oil

½ tsp dry Italian seasoning

½ tsp red pepper flakes

1 cup/240 ml red wine

8 large shrimp/prawns

8 fresh clams

8 crab claws

Crush the whole tomatoes with your hands to break them apart slightly. Peel and finely chop the onion and garlic. Clean and debeard the mussels (see Cooking Tip, below). Cut the salmon into chunks 2 in/5 cm long.

Put the olive oil in a large saucepan over medium-high heat. Add the onion and cook, stirring occasionally, for 5 minutes, or until translucent. Add the garlic and cook, stirring constantly for 1 minute. Add the crushed tomatoes, Italian seasoning, and red pepper flakes and bring to a boil. Add the wine, reduce the heat to medium-low, and cook, stirring occasionally, for 20 minutes to meld the flavors. (You can stop at this point and reheat the sauce later.)

Gently stir in the shrimp/prawns, clams, mussels, crab claws, and salmon and increase the heat to high. Cover, bring to a boil, and cook for 2 minutes, or just until the shellfish begin to open. Remove from the heat, spoon the cioppino into four bowls, and serve immediately.

Cooking Tip

Cleaning and "debearding," or removing the hairy fibers that stick out of mussel shells, sounds like a big deal, but it's really not. To clean the mussels, soak them in a bowl of cold water for 20 minutes. As the mussels breathe, they will expel salt and sand. Discard any that have broken or chipped shells or are not tightly closed. Remove the mussels from the water one at a time and hold firmly. Using a dry towel, grasp the dry fibers that are sticking out of the shell and pull down sharply toward the hinge end of the mussel (the wider end). Clean any dirt off the shells using a vegetable brush and put them in a bowl of clean water as you finish debearding them. When you are finished debearding, remove the mussels from the water (don't pour them out into a strainer, or the sand will end up back in the mussels) and dry them off before cooking.

CLAM CHOWDER

Megan

To me, clam chowder is this thick, creamy, hearty soup with potatoes, vegetables, and, of course, clams. But there are countless variations on this classic New England dish, some of which include tomatoes and are broth based. The good news is the state of Maine has it under control. At least they did when they made it illegal to put tomatoes in clam chowder. I don't know if that law is still in effect today, but I know I won't ever let tomatoes get anywhere near my clam chowder.

2 stalks celery

1 small onion

1 russet potato

¼ cup/55 g butter

¼ cup/30 g flour

One 8-oz/240-ml bottle clam juice

Two 6.5-oz/185-g cans minced clams, juices reserved

2 cups/480 ml chicken or vegetable broth

2 cups/480 ml milk

Salt and pepper

Cut the celery into pieces ¼ in/6 mm long. Peel the onion and cut it into pieces ¼ in/6 mm wide. Peel the potato and dice it into cubes ¼ in/6 mm wide.

Melt the butter in a large saucepan, add the celery, onion, and potato, and cook over medium heat, stirring occasionally, for 10 minutes, or until the onion is softened. Add the flour to the pan and stir constantly, until the mixture has bubbled for 1 minute. Slowly stir in the clam juice, the clams with their juice, broth, and milk, and season with salt and pepper. Cook over medium heat for 10 minutes, or until hot. Serve immediately.

SHRIMP ÉTOUFFÉE

Megan

I love spicy food! Somehow the feeling or not-feeling of my mouth when it is burning from super-spicy food makes me feel alive. Maybe it's the adrenaline rush that chiles give you when you eat them. In any case, this spicy Cajun stew is one of my new favorites! Even though I am the queen of my kitchen, I try to remember that not everybody likes to cry at dinner, so I toned this one down a little. You can put hot sauce or red pepper flakes on the table for the more adventurous eaters.

1 small yellow onion

1 stalk celery

½ red bell pepper/capsicum

4 green/spring onions

2 large tomatoes

1 clove garlic

1 lb/455 g shrimp/prawns

¼ cup/55 g butter

2 tbsp Cajun seasoning

¼ cup/30 g flour

1½ cups/360 ml chicken broth

2 tsp Worcestershire sauce

½ tsp dried thyme

2 tbsp chopped fresh parsley

1 cup/215 g dry white rice

2¼ cups/540 ml water

Peel the yellow onion and chop it into pieces ¼ in/6 mm thick. Cut the celery and red bell pepper/capsicum into pieces ¼ in/6 mm thick. Thinly slice the white and light green parts of the green/spring onions. Cut the tomatoes into pieces ½ in/12 mm wide. Peel and finely chop the garlic. Peel the shrimp/prawns.

Melt the butter in a large frying pan over medium heat. Add the yellow onion, red bell pepper/capsicum, and celery and cook for 10 minutes, or until the vegetables are soft. Add the Cajun seasoning and flour and cook, stirring constantly, for 2 minutes. Slowly add the broth, stirring constantly until the sauce is smooth. Bring to a boil, stirring frequently. Reduce the heat to medium-low and add the tomatoes, garlic, Worcestershire sauce, and thyme. Simmer, stirring occasionally, for 30 minutes. Add the shrimp/prawns, green/spring onions, and parsley and simmer for 5 minutes more, or until the shellfish turn pink and begin to curl up.

Meanwhile, put the rice and water in a small saucepan and bring to a boil. Cover and cook over low heat for 20 minutes, or until tender.

Spoon the rice onto four plates, top with the étouffée, and serve immediately.

MOULES-FRITES (STEAMED MUSSELS WITH FRENCH FRIES)

Jill

Mussels and fries are a classic French combination. When I studied in France, the city I lived in had a huge flea market every year. During the weeks this flea market was going on, all the mussel restaurants (yes, there was more than one) had a contest to see who could sell the most mussels. How did they know who sold the most you ask? Maybe comparing sales or purchase records? No, they took all the empty shells and stacked them up in a giant pile in front of the restaurant. Whoever had the biggest pile obviously sold the most mussels and thus won eternal glory in the mussel hall of fame.

FRENCH FRIES

2 lb/910 g russet potatoes (4 or 5)

2 tbsp canola oil

Salt and pepper

MUSSELS

3 to 4 lb/1.4 to 1.8 kg fresh mussels

1 small onion

4 cloves garlic

2 tbsp olive oil

1 cup/240 ml white wine

¼ cup/10 g finely chopped fresh parsley

Salt and pepper

To prepare the French fries: Preheat the oven to 400°F/200°C/gas mark 6.

Peel the potatoes and cut them into sticks ¼ in/6mm wide. Soak the potatoes in cold water for 15 minutes to remove some of the starch. Strain and dry completely with paper towels/absorbent paper. Put the potatoes on a baking sheet/tray and drizzle with the canola oil. Toss the potatoes until they are completely coated, season with salt and pepper, and bake for 30 minutes, or until lightly browned and crispy.

To prepare the mussels: Clean the mussels (see Cooking Tips, page 70).

Peel and finely chop the onion and garlic. Put the olive oil in a large saucepan over medium-high heat. Add the onion and cook, stirring frequently, for 5 minutes, or until soft. Add the garlic, wine, and parsley and season with salt and pepper. Bring to a boil, add the mussels, and cover immediately. Cook for 2 minutes and check to see if the mussels have opened. If not, cook for 1 minute more and discard any shells that have not opened. Do not cook longer than 3 minutes total, or the mussels can get tough. Serve immediately with the French fries on the side.

variation STEAMED MUSSELS IN MARINARA SAUCE

Follow the cooking directions, decreasing the wine to ½ cup/120 ml and adding ½ tsp red pepper flakes with the garlic. Once the mussels have opened, add 3 cups/720 ml Marinara Sauce (page 43) and cook, uncovered for 2 to 3 minutes, or until the sauce is hot.

SHRIMP PO' BOY WITH CAJUN FRIES

Jill

I make these Cajun fries in the oven instead of frying them for two reasons: First, oven-baked fries/chips are lower in calories and, even though the shrimp/prawns are fried, I figure every little bit helps. Second, the shellfish can fry in about 1 in/2.5 cm of oil. The French fries need at least three times that much. That means that I not only have to buy three times as much oil, I have to figure out how to get rid of it when I'm finished. If you don't care about either of those issues, then fry away—but put the seasoning on after cooking instead of before.

CAJUN FRIES

2 lb/910 g russet potatoes (4 or 5)

2 tbsp canola oil

1 tbsp Cajun seasoning

SHRIMP PO' BOY

1 lb/455 g medium shrimp/prawns

One 1-lb/455-g French baguette

1 large tomato

¼ cup/60 ml mayonnaise

1 cup/ 70 g shredded iceberg lettuce

Canola oil, for frying

1 egg

½ cup/60 g flour

¼ cup/35 g cornmeal

1 tbsp Cajun seasoning

½ tsp salt

Hot sauce, for serving

To prepare the Cajun fries: Preheat the oven to 400°F/200°C/gas mark 6.

Cut each potato into eight wedges and put them on a baking sheet/tray. Drizzle with the canola oil and sprinkle with the Cajun seasoning. Toss until completely coated and bake for 45 minutes, or until lightly browned and crispy.

To prepare the shrimp po' boy: Peel the shrimp/prawns. Cut the baguette into four chunks and slice open each piece, leaving the bread hinged on one side. Cut the tomato into eight thin slices.

Lay open the pieces of bread and spread the entire inside with the mayonnaise. Place the lettuce on one half of each piece of bread and top with two tomato slices.

Pour about 1 in/2.5 cm of oil into a large saucepan, leaving at least 4 in/10 cm at the top of the pan to allow for the oil to bubble up during cooking. Put over high heat until very hot (about 375°F/190°C on a deep-fat thermometer). A small drop of water added to the pan should immediately begin to bubble.

Beat the egg in a bowl with 2 tbsp water until combined. Put the flour, cornmeal, the 1 tbsp Cajun seasoning, and the salt in a resealable bag and shake to mix well. Put all the shrimp/prawns in the egg and stir until completely coated. Put some of the shellfish in the bag and shake until thoroughly coated.

(continued)

Carefully add to the hot oil and cook for 3 to 4 minutes, or until golden brown. Do not overcrowd the pan or they will cook too slowly and become greasy. Drain on paper towels/absorbent paper and repeat with the remaining prawns.

Place the cooked shrimp/prawns on the sandwiches and serve with the Cajun Fries and hot sauce on the side.

Cooking Tip

When deep frying, always use a pot that is at least 4 in/10 cm deeper than the amount of oil. This allows room for the oil to bubble up without going over the sides of the pan and causing a grease fire. In the unlikely event that you do have a grease fire, immediately turn off the burner and put a metal lid on the pan. If you don't have a lid, you can douse the fire with baking soda/bicarbonate of soda. DO NOT USE WATER OR A HOME FIRE EXTINGUISHER. Water causes the oil to bubble more and the force from the extinguisher causes the oil to spray all over and the fire to spread.

BLTS (BACON, LETTUCE, TOMATO, AND SALMON) WITH CUCUMBER SALAD

Jill

I swear I get my best ideas just staring into the refrigerator. I was thinking about making a BLT one day but was looking around for other targets of opportunity when I saw some leftover salmon from the night before. Next thing you know, I had my first BLTS and it was fabulous, if I do say so myself. This is a great way to use up leftover salmon, but it's worth the trouble to cook some just to make these sandwiches.

CUCUMBER SALAD

3 cucumbers

1 small onion

½ cup/120 ml sour cream

Salt and pepper

BLTS

8 slices bacon/streaky bacon

¼ cup/60 ml mayonnaise

1 tbsp fresh lemon juice

1 large tomato

8 slices bread

8 oz/225 g salmon fillet, skin removed

1 clove garlic

1 cup/30 g loosely packed mixed greens

To prepare the cucumber salad: Peel the cucumbers and onion and thinly slice them. Put the cucumbers, onion, and sour cream in a bowl and stir until combined. Season with salt and pepper and refrigerate until ready to serve.

To prepare the BLTs: Put the bacon in a large frying pan and cook over medium-high heat, turning occasionally for 15 minutes, or until crisp. Remove the bacon from the pan and drain on paper towels/absorbent paper. Drain the bacon grease from the pan, leaving just a coating on the bottom.

Combine the mayonnaise and lemon juice in a small bowl. Cut the tomato into eight thin slices. Toast the bread.

Add the salmon and unpeeled garlic to the hot bacon pan and cook over medium heat for 3 to 4 minutes on each side, or until cooked through. Remove the garlic from the pan and peel. Smash the garlic and mix it into the mayonnaise mixture.

Place one piece of toast on each plate and top with two pieces of bacon. Arrange the greens and tomato over the bacon and top with a piece of salmon. Spoon some of the mayonnaise on the salmon, then top with the remaining pieces of bread. Serve immediately with the salad on the side.

Cooking Tip

To dispose of the oil from cooked bacon or from frying, let it cool completely, pour it into an empty container, and cover tightly. Never pour oil down the drain. When it hits the cold pipes, it will become solid and clog them.

OVEN-BAKED FISH AND CHIPS

 Megan

Although English cuisine is not looked upon in a particularly good light, there is no denying that perfectly cooked fish and chips or "fish fry," as we traitors like to call it, is the No. 1 pub food. I decided to make this version of fish and chips in the oven, which not only saves your house from that fried smell, but saves quite a few calories, too! I use panko bread crumbs because they are larger and crunchier than normal bread crumbs and make the perfectly crisp coating that fried fish should have.

TARTAR SAUCE

½ cup/120 ml mayonnaise

¼ cup/60 ml pickle relish or chopped pickles

1 tbsp fresh lemon juice

1 tbsp finely chopped onion

CHIPS

2 lb/910 g russet potatoes (4 or 5)

2 tbsp canola oil

Salt and pepper

FISH

Cooking spray

½ cup/60 g flour

Salt and pepper

1 egg

2 cups/120 g panko bread crumbs

1 lb/455 g tilapia or cod fillets

To prepare the tartar sauce: Combine the mayonnaise, pickle relish, lemon juice, and onion in a small bowl and refrigerate until ready to serve.

Preheat the oven to 400°F/200°C/gas mark 6.

To prepare the chips: Cut each potato into eight wedges and place them on a baking sheet/tray. Drizzle with the canola oil and toss until completely coated. Season with salt and pepper and bake for 45 minutes, or until lightly browned and crispy.

To prepare the fish: Lightly coat a baking sheet/tray with cooking spray or oil. Put the flour in a shallow bowl and season with salt and pepper. Beat the egg in a bowl with 2 tbsp water until combined. Put the bread crumbs in a third bowl. Cut the tilapia fillets in half lengthwise, then again widthwise. Dredge the pieces of fish in the flour, then the egg, then the bread crumbs, and put them on the prepared baking sheet/tray. Spray the fish generously with cooking spray and bake for 15 minutes, or until lightly browned.

Place some of the fish and potato wedges on each plate and serve with the tartar sauce on the side.

 *Lingo*

Dredge means to coat food lightly in something dry, such as flour, bread crumbs, or cornmeal. It's like dipping, but for dry ingredients.

MEDITERRANEAN COD WITH RICE

Megan

There has been all this talk over the last ten years about the Mediterranean diet and how it is so good for you, but the question I always ask myself is, "What is the Mediterranean diet? What do they eat that is so special?" In my travels, I have seen lots of "Mediterranean food," which I found meant lots of fresh ingredients and flavorful herbs like bell peppers/capsicums, tomatoes, zucchini/courgette, eggplant/aubergine, thyme, rosemary, and, most important, lots of garlic and olive oil. This recipe combines some of those ingredients with cod, a mild white fish that picks up all the great flavors to make a delicious, light, and healthful "Mediterranean" dish.

RICE

1 cup/215 g dry white rice

2¼ cups/540 ml water

MEDITERRANEAN COD

8 oz/225 g fresh mushrooms

1 small onion

2 cloves garlic

2 tbsp olive oil

One 2-oz/55-g can sliced ripe olives

Two 15-oz/430-g cans whole tomatoes, juices reserved

½ tsp dry Italian seasoning

Salt and pepper

1 lb/455 g cod fillets

To prepare the rice: Put the rice and water in a small saucepan and bring to a boil. Cover and cook over low heat for 20 minutes, or until tender. Keep warm.

To prepare the Mediterranean Cod: Remove the stem ends from the mushrooms and slice the caps. Peel, halve, and thinly slice the onion. Peel and finely chop the garlic.

Put the olive oil in a large saucepan over medium-high heat. Add the mushrooms and onion and cook for 10 minutes, or until the onion is soft. Add the garlic, olives, tomatoes with the juice, and the Italian seasoning, and season with salt and pepper. Using the side of a spoon, cut the tomatoes in half and cook, stirring occasionally, for 10 minutes.

Cut the cod into pieces 2 in/5 cm wide and add them to the pan, pushing them partway down into the liquid. Cover and cook for 10 minutes, or until the cod is flaky. Serve immediately over the rice.

On the Lighter Side

Here's another flavor-packed low-calorie dish. It has about 360 calories per serving with more than 30 g of protein and only 11 g of fat. This is the kind of meal that makes you forget you're watching what you eat.

HONEY-CITRUS GLAZED SALMON WITH CARAMELIZED ONION MASHED POTATOES

 Jill

The nice part about salmon is that it can be prepared so many different ways. It takes on the flavor of the marinade, yet still retains its own flavor. A more delicately flavored fish would be completely overpowered. This marinade is slightly sweet and, paired with the caramelized onion mashed potatoes, it makes a fabulous meal.

MASHED POTATOES

1 large onion

6 tbsp/85 g butter

2 lb/910 g russet potatoes (4 or 5)

½ cup/120 ml milk

Salt and pepper

SALMON

1 orange

¼ cup/60 ml honey

Four 5- to 6-oz/140- to 170-g salmon fillets

To prepare the mashed potatoes: Peel, halve, and cut the onion into slices ¼ in/6 mm thick. Melt 2 tbsp/30 g of the butter in a frying pan and add the onion. Cook over medium-high heat, stirring occasionally, for 15 minutes, or until golden brown.

Peel the potatoes and cut them into medium chunks. Put the potatoes in a saucepan of salted water and cook over medium heat for 20 to 30 minutes, or until soft. Drain off the water and return the pan to the stove. Add the remaining ¼ cup/55 g butter and the milk to the pan and cook over medium heat until the milk comes to a boil. Smash the potatoes with a fork or potato masher until fairly smooth, stir in the caramelized onions, and season with salt and pepper.

To prepare the salmon: Preheat the oven to 350°F/180°C/gas mark 4.

Finely grate the zest of the orange and put it in a small glass bowl. Squeeze the juice from the orange and add it to the bowl. Add the honey and microwave on high heat for 30 seconds to soften the honey. Stir until combined. Put the salmon fillets in a foil-lined baking pan and brush with the glaze. Bake the salmon for 12 to 15 minutes, or until the insides of the salmon are just barely translucent.

Put the remaining glaze in a microwave-safe bowl and heat for 1 minute, or until warm.

Place one salmon fillet on each plate and spoon on the remaining sauce. Place some of the potatoes on each plate and serve immediately.

 Lingo

Zest is what the colored outside of citrus fruit is called once is has been peeled or grated. You can get special tools for this, but the fine side of a box grater works just as well. Be careful not to get to the white pith that is under the zest when grating because it is bitter.

TERIYAKI SALMON WITH JASMINE RICE

Jill

You have to love a dish with five ingredients, including water. This is a really easy way to prepare salmon, and it's delicious. I made this one night when I had some friends coming over. I later found out that one of them didn't like salmon . . . until she tried this. Another convert! My day was complete.

SALMON

1 cup/240 ml teriyaki sauce

1 tsp finely chopped peeled fresh ginger

Four 5- to 6-oz/140- to 170-g skinless salmon fillets

RICE

1 cup/215 g jasmine rice

2¼ cups/540 ml water

To prepare the salmon: Combine the teriyaki sauce and ginger in a small bowl. Put ½ cup/120 ml of the sauce in a resealable bag and add the salmon fillets. Refrigerate for 1 hour, turning occasionally.

To prepare the rice: Put the rice and water in a small saucepan and bring to a boil. Cover and cook over medium-low heat for 15 minutes, or until the rice is tender.

Preheat a grill/barbecue or grill pan on high heat. Put the salmon on the grill and cook for 5 minutes. Turn over with a spatula and cook for 3 to 4 minutes, or until the inside of the salmon is just barely translucent.

Put the remaining sauce in a microwave-safe bowl and cook on high for 1 minute, or until warm.

Spoon some of the rice onto each plate and top with a salmon fillet. Spoon some of the sauce over the salmon and rice and serve immediately.

Ingredient Info

Fresh ginger always seems to come in larger pieces than you need. When you have extra, cut the pieces into 1-in/2.5-cm chunks, put them in a resealable bag, and put it in the freezer. Next time you need ginger, you can thaw what you need and use it as directed.

MACADAMIA NUT–CRUSTED MAHI MAHI WITH FRUIT SALSA

Jill

Mahi mahi is a weird looking fish. Seriously, look it up. They almost look like miniature versions of whales. That said, you will probably never see them in one piece if, like me, you live in a landlocked state. You can get mahi mahi and other fish in the frozen food section or in the meat section of your grocery store. Don't be fooled by things that say "fresh," though, because most fish that we landlocked people get has been frozen at one point or another. If you are lucky enough to live near the ocean, take advantage of all the nice seafood you have and try this.

SALSA

1 mango

½ fresh, ripe pineapple

1 jalapeño pepper

¼ cup/30 g finely diced red onion

1 lime

Salt and pepper

MAHI MAHI

1¼ cups/740 g finely chopped macadamia nuts

1¼ cups/140 g panko bread crumbs

¾ cup/170 g butter, melted

⅓ cup/40 g shredded/dessicated coconut

Four 6-oz/170-g mahi mahi fillets

2 tbsp canola oil

To prepare the salsa: Peel the mango, cut it into pieces ¼ to ½ in/6 to 12 mm thick, and put them in a bowl. Peel the pineapple and cut it off of the core. Cut the pineapple into pieces ¼ to ½ in/6 to 12 mm thick and add them to the bowl. Halve, seed, and finely chop the jalapeño. Add the jalapeño and onion to the bowl. Grate the zest from the lime and add it to the bowl. Squeeze the juice from the lime into the bowl and stir until combined. Season with salt and pepper and refrigerate for at least 1 hour before serving.

To prepare the mahi mahi: Combine the nuts, bread crumbs, butter, and coconut in a bowl. Put the mahi mahi fillets on a plate and spoon some of the bread crumb mixture on each one. Firmly pat the bread crumbs to evenly coat both sides of the fish. Cover with plastic wrap/cling film and refrigerate for 30 minutes, or until the butter is hard.

Put the canola oil in a large frying pan over medium heat. Add the mahi mahi and cook for 5 to 6 minutes on each side, or until the centers are no longer translucent. Place a piece of mahi mahi on each plate and spoon some of the fruit salsa on the side. Serve immediately.

> ## Ingredient Info

Limes can often be kind of dry and hard to juice. If you put them in the microwave for 10 or 15 seconds on high, it softens them up, making them much easier to juice.

PECAN-CRUSTED TROUT WITH WARM GREEN BEAN–TOMATO SALAD

Megan I think trout is too often overlooked in the seafood department. Not only can it be prepared in a ton of different ways, but it has more flavor than most white fish. In this recipe, I use fillets, but if you wanted to experiment a bit you could try making a whole fish. My newest favorite is prepared with a whole trout that is marinated with olive oil, garlic, salt, and pepper and then slowly roasted on a stick over the grill/barbecue.

TROUT

¾ cup/85 g pecans

¾ cup/85 g dry bread crumbs

¼ cup/10 g chopped fresh parsley

8 trout or flounder fillets
(about 1½ lb/680 g)

1 lemon, juiced

Salt and pepper

SALAD

2 cups/280 g grape tomatoes

2 tbsp balsamic vinegar

8 oz/225 g fresh green beans

1 small shallot

Salt and pepper

To prepare the trout: Preheat the oven to 400°F/200°C/gas mark 6.

Put the pecans in a baking pan/tin and bake for 5 minutes, or until lightly browned. Put the pecans in a blender with the bread crumbs and pulse until finely ground. Put the nut mixture and the parsley in a bowl and stir until combined.

Put the trout on a foil-lined baking sheet/tray, drizzle with the lemon juice, and season with salt and pepper. Spoon the pecan mixture over the fish and gently press it down to evenly coat the fish. Bake for 15 minutes, or until the trout is firm and flaky.

To prepare the salad: Put the grape tomatoes in a small baking dish and toss with 1 tbsp of the vinegar. Bake for 10 minutes, or until the tomatoes begin to soften.

Cut the green beans into pieces 1 in/2.5 cm long. Bring a saucepan of salted water to a boil and add the green beans. Cook for 5 minutes, or until bright green and tender-crisp. Drain the beans and keep warm. Peel and finely chop the shallot. Add the shallot and remaining 1 tbsp vinegar to the green beans and stir until combined. Season with salt and pepper and gently stir in the tomatoes, being careful not to smash them.

Place two trout fillets on each plate and spoon some of the green bean–tomato salad alongside the fish. Serve immediately.

> ## Ingredient Info
>
> Balsamic vinegar has a rich, slightly sweet flavor that is completely different from any other vinegar. It is pressed from unfermented grapes and then aged in wooden casks. As it ages, it is moved to casks made from different types of wood, each adding their own flavor. The longer it ages, the sweeter, richer, and more expensive it becomes. One-hundred-year-old balsamic from Modena, Italy, can cost an exorbitant amount for a 3-oz/90-ml bottle. Assuming that it is priced out of your budget, look for a commercial version that has no added sweeteners or caramel color.

Chapter

CHICKEN

Chicken is by far the most commonly used poultry. Its low fat content, cholesterol, and calories make it a healthful choice, and its neutral flavor makes it extremely versatile. It works well with all types of marinades, spices, or sauces and with almost any cooking technique. Chickens can be purchased whole, cut in pieces, or boneless. We opt for buying the pieces we need for the dish. We know how to cut up a whole chicken; we just don't like to. Thankfully for us, the pieces often go on sale for less than the whole chickens. But, if you like cutting up chickens, it's usually more economical.

Any chef will tell you that making your own stocks from scratch is the only way to go. We agree . . . sort of. Homemade stock is delicious, and in a perfect world we would all have homemade stock in our freezers, but, the reality is there are times when it's just not convenient. The key is knowing when you really need homemade and when it's okay to substitute the canned version. When you're making soups or stews like the ones that follow, it makes sense to make the stock from scratch because you want the extra richness of the homemade version. If you are adding a cup of stock to a dish with other flavors going on, it's not going to make a difference.

That said, making a stock or broth is something everyone should know how to do. They are all made the same way. It doesn't matter whether you are using beef, veal, or chicken. There are two basic methods: using bones or using meat. If you just use bones, it is called a stock. The bones are roasted for 30 minutes and then cooked for about 4 hours. If you use meat, it is technically a broth, and it only needs to cook for about an hour because the meat adds flavor more quickly. We use a combination of the two—meat and bones with the shorter cooking time—and call it broth. Either way, they are interchangeable.

There are a few rules to making a successful broth.

Always start with cold liquid. Adding warm water to meat quickly releases the soluble proteins in the meat. That means your broth will end up cloudy and no amount of straining will clear it up. Using cold water causes the proteins to release slowly and in larger clumps that float to the top of the pan where they can be skimmed off.

Don't stir the broth while it's cooking. Stirring pushes the proteins back into the liquid, causing it to become cloudy.

Don't allow the broth to boil. Again, the agitation of boiling causes the proteins to mix back into the broth instead of floating to the top. It should just maintain a gentle simmer.

BASIC CHICKEN BROTH

MAKES ABOUT 2 QT/2 L

This recipe is just what is says, basic. We didn't add any herbs or extra vegetables to alter the flavor. That way, if you don't need all of it you can freeze the extra for another use. We tell you in the directions to discard the chicken that is cooked in the broth. Any chef will tell you not to use it because most of the flavor from the chicken is in the broth. That's true, but I'm not a chef. I'm a grad student on a budget, so I often use it in soup or for Chicken and Dumplings (page 95) or Upside-Down Chicken Pot Pie (page 101) where you won't notice it as much. If your budget isn't an issue, by all means, throw it away. Otherwise use it where it will be least noticeable. It's your choice.

2 onions

4 stalks celery

2 lb/910 g chicken pieces with bones

2 tsp salt

Peel and quarter the onions. Wash the celery, leaving the leaves on, and cut each stalk into four pieces. Put the onions, celery, chicken, and salt in a stock pot and add 10 cups/2.4 L cold water. Bring the stock to a simmer and cook over medium-low heat for 1 hour, skimming the impurities from the top two or three times during cooking.

Strain the broth through a fine-mesh sieve, discarding the vegetables and chicken (or not, as noted above). Cool slightly and refrigerate the broth until ready to use. Before using, skim off any fat that has risen to the top.

CHICKEN NOODLE SOUP

Jill

I made good, old-fashioned chicken noodle soup here, but feel free to change it to your taste. You can use rice instead of noodles, add other vegetables, or add herbs to give it a little different flavor.

1 small onion

2 carrots

2 stalks celery

8 cups/2 L Basic Chicken Broth (page 89)

Salt and pepper

8 oz/225 g boneless, skinless chicken

1½ cups/85 g dry noodles

½ tsp ground nutmeg

Peel the onion and cut it into pieces ½ in/12 mm long. Peel the carrots and cut them into discs ¼ in/6 mm thick. Trim the celery and cut it into slices ¼ in/6 mm thick.

Put the broth in a large saucepan. Add the onion, carrots, and celery and bring to a simmer. Cook over medium heat for 15 minutes or until the vegetables just start to soften. Season with salt and pepper. Cut the chicken into bite-size pieces. Add the chicken and noodles to the pan and cook over medium-high heat for 10 minutes. Add the nutmeg and cook for 5 minutes, or until the noodles are soft. Serve immediately.

variation CHICKEN, PENNE, AND SNAP PEA SOUP

Follow the directions above, reducing the broth to 7 cups/1.7 L, the chicken to 4 oz/115 g, substituting 1 cup/115 g dry penne pasta for the noodles, and omitting the nutmeg. When the pasta is cooked, add 1 cup/70 g fresh snap peas. Stir together ¼ cup/30 g flour and ½ cup/120 ml water until completely smooth. Slowly stir the mixture into the finished soup and cook for 2 minutes, or until it just begins to bubble. Top with 1 tbsp chopped fresh parsley and serve immediately.

MATZO BALL SOUP

Megan

If you have never seen a matzo ball before, imagine a golf ball made out of crackers—you've got it! It may sound a little strange, but it's delicious and way more fun than noodles. This is a great light meal that is perfect for lunch or dinner—or both! I often make soup for myself and save the leftovers for lunch the next day. It's easy to reheat, and it's nice and light.

2 tbsp canola oil

2 large eggs

½ cup/55 g matzo meal

Salt

8 cups/2 L Basic Chicken Broth (page 89)

Pepper

Put the canola oil and eggs in a small bowl and whisk until completely combined. Add the matzo meal and 1 tsp salt and stir well. Add 2 tbsp of the broth and mix until thoroughly combined. Refrigerate for 15 minutes.

Meanwhile, pour the remaining broth into a large saucepan and bring it to a boil. Season with salt and pepper. Form the matzo dough into balls 1 in/2.5 cm in diameter and drop them into the boiling broth. Cover and cook over medium heat for 15 minutes, or until the matzo balls have puffed up and are floating on the top of the soup. Serve immediately.

AVGOLEMONO SOUP
(GREEK LEMON-EGG SOUP)

Megan

I first tried this when I started working at a Greek restaurant. I thought it was cream of chicken soup until I tried it. The tart lemony flavor surprised me at first, but soon I was sneaking a little taste every chance I got! The interesting thing is that it isn't thickened with a roux, like soups often are, but with egg and cornstarch/cornflour like an Asian soup.

6 cups/1.4 L Basic Chicken Broth (page 89)

¼ cup/50 g dry rice

1 cup/240 ml milk

3 large egg yolks

1 tbsp cornstarch/cornflour

¼ cup/60 ml fresh lemon juice

2 tbsp chopped fresh parsley

Put the broth in a large saucepan and bring it to a boil. Stir in the rice, cover, and cook over medium heat for 20 minutes, or until the rice is tender.

Put the milk, egg yolks, and cornstarch/cornflour in a bowl and whisk until thoroughly combined. Remove the pan from the heat and slowly pour the egg mixture into the soup, whisking constantly. Return the pan to the heat and cook, stirring constantly, for 2 minutes, or until slightly thickened. Remove from the heat, stir in the lemon juice and parsley, and serve immediately.

TORTILLA SOUP

Jill

Tortilla soup is one of those things I used to order in restaurants but never tried to make at home. It has so much stuff in it I thought it would be pretty complicated. Once I figured out that most of those things came in cans, I started making it all the time. That way I can make extra tortilla strips and have as many as I want.

4 corn tortillas

2 tbsp canola oil

Salt

1 small onion

1 clove garlic

4 cups/960 ml Basic Chicken Broth (page 89)

One 15-oz/430-g can diced tomatoes, juice reserved

One 4-oz/115-g can chopped green chiles, juice reserved

One 15-oz/430-g can black beans

One 15-oz/430-g can corn

1 cup/150 g cooked, shredded chicken

1 tbsp Mexican seasoning or chili powder

Pepper

1 cup/115 g shredded Jack cheese

Preheat the oven to 375°F/190°C/gas mark 5.

Cut the tortillas into strips ¼ in/6 mm wide and toss with 1 tbsp of the canola oil. Spread the strips on a baking sheet/tray, sprinkle with salt, and bake for 10 minutes, or until crisp.

Meanwhile, peel the onion and cut it into pieces ½ in/12 mm long. Put the onion in a large saucepan with the remaining 1 tbsp of oil and cook over medium-high heat, stirring frequently, for 8 minutes, or until lightly browned. Peel and finely chop the garlic. Add it to the pan and cook, stirring constantly, for 30 seconds.

Add the broth, tomatoes with their juice, and chiles with their juice. Drain the beans and corn and add them to the pan. Stir in the chicken and Mexican seasoning and season with salt and pepper. Cook over medium heat for 20 minutes, or until hot. Ladle the soup into bowls and top with the tortilla strips and cheese. Serve immediately.

There are several ways to thicken sauces. Deciding which method to use depends on the situation. One way is to combine cornstarch/cornflour and water to create a slurry. Cornstarch/cornflour is a great thickener that leaves the sauce translucent and, as long as it's mixed with water first, always produces a smooth sauce. Unfortunately, it doesn't have a lot of staying power. If you cook it for longer than 10 minutes, it begins to lose its thickening power and your sauce can turn runny. But if you're adding it at the end, it is a good choice for this dish.

If you need to cook a sauce longer than that, you are better off using a flour and water slurry or a *roux* (pronounced "rue"). Flour slurries work the same as the cornstarch/cornflour, but they make the sauce opaque, and they can handle long cook times. The downside of flour slurries is that they can cause lumps. Make sure that the slurry is completely smooth and runny and stir constantly as you slowly pour it into the hot liquid. If you don't stir it as it goes in, you are almost guaranteed to get lumps, and, once you have lumps, the only way to get them out is with a strainer.

A roux is equal parts of butter and flour that are cooked together in the pan before the liquid is added. The amount of cooking time depends on the end result you are looking for. For a white sauce, you cook it for only 1 or 2 minutes, or until it has bubbled for a minute or so. If you are making a gumbo, the roux will cook for about 20 minutes, until it is dark brown and has a nutty aroma. The key to making a smooth sauce with a roux is adding the liquid a little at a time at the beginning and stirring until smooth after each addition. For example, if you're adding 8 cups/2 L of liquid, start with 1 cup/240 ml and stir until smooth. Add another 1 cup/240 ml and stir well. That will loosen up the roux enough to allow you to add the remaining liquid all at once and have a smooth sauce. Don't panic if you added the liquid too quickly and have lumps—just get out a whisk and stir vigorously for a couple of minutes to smooth it out. It's not a mistake; it's kitchen aerobics!

CHICKEN AND DUMPLINGS

Jill

Chicken and dumplings can have two kinds of dumplings: light, fluffy drop dumplings that sit on top of the chicken; or dense, cut dumplings that get mixed in with the chicken. We've always made the fluffy dumplings, so that's what this recipe uses. If the cut dumplings sound good, you can combine 2 cups/255 g of flour, ½ tsp baking soda/ bicarbonate of soda, 3 tbsp softened butter, and ¾ cup/180 ml milk; roll the dough out about ½ in/12 mm thick on a floured board; and cut into 1-in/2.5-cm squares.

1 onion

2 carrots

2 stalks celery

2 red potatoes

1 lb/455 g boneless, skinless chicken

5 cups/1.2 L Basic Chicken Broth (page 89)

Salt and pepper

1⅓ cups/155 g flour

½ cup/120 ml milk

1½ tsp baking powder

Peel the onion and cut it into pieces ½ in/12 mm long. Peel the carrots and cut them into discs ¼ in/6 mm thick. Trim the celery and cut the stalks into slices ¼ in/6 mm thick. Peel the potatoes and cut them into chunks 1 in/2.5 cm thick. Cut the chicken into bite-size pieces.

Put the broth in a large saucepan. Add the chicken, onion, carrots, celery, and potatoes and cook over medium heat for 15 minutes or until the potatoes just begin to soften. Season with salt and pepper.

Stir together ⅓ cup/40 g of the flour and ½ cup/120 ml water and slowly pour the mixture into the pan, stirring constantly. Cook over medium heat until it just begins to bubble.

Put the remaining 1 cup/115 g flour, the milk, baking powder, and ½ tsp salt in a bowl and stir until they are completely combined. Drop heaping spoonfuls of the mixture into the soup and cook, uncovered, for 5 minutes, or until they begin to fluff up. Cover the pan and cook for 10 minutes more, or until the dumplings are dry on top. (If the sauce has bubbled up over the dumplings, insert a knife in the largest one to make sure it is cooked through.) Serve immediately.

BARBECUE CHICKEN SALAD

Jill

I have a problem. It's true. I have an addiction to barbecue chicken salads. I have eaten them at probably every restaurant that sells them and have made them at home more often than I care to admit. Being a connoisseur of barbecue chicken salad, I have come to find that the best ones, in my opinion, have jicama. It seems kind of weird when you're cutting it up, but it is a nice, crunchy contrast to the corn and chicken. If you like black beans or tortilla strips in your salad, you can add those, too.

1 lb/455 g boneless, skinless chicken breasts (2 or 3)

¾ cup/180 ml barbecue sauce

1 head romaine/Cos lettuce

2 tomatoes

½ small jicama

One 15-oz/430-g can corn

¼ cup/60 ml mayonnaise

¾ cup roughly chopped cilantro/fresh coriander

Preheat a grill/barbecue or grill pan on high heat.

Put the chicken on the grill/barbecue and cook, turning occasionally, for 10 minutes, or until it is cooked through. Remove the chicken from the grill, cool slightly, and cut it into ½ in-by-½ in/12 mm-by-12 mm cubes. Combine the chicken and ½ cup/120 ml of the barbecue sauce in a bowl and set aside.

Cut the lettuce into bite-size pieces. Halve, seed, and cut the tomatoes into pieces ½ in/12 mm long. Peel the jicama and cut it into ½-by-½-in/12-by-12-mm cubes. Drain the corn.

Combine the remaining ¼ cup/60 ml of the barbecue sauce with the mayonnaise in a small bowl. (If it is too thick, add 1 tbsp milk to thin it.)

Place some of the lettuce on each plate. Sprinkle the tomato, cilantro/fresh coriander, jicama, and corn over the lettuce and top with the barbecue chicken. Serve immediately with the dressing on the side.

BUFFALO CHICKEN WRAP

Megan

When you buy wraps on the go, they can cost more than you want to pay. If you buy the ingredients and make them to take along, you can put whatever you want in them, and they cost about one quarter of the price. In this buffalo chicken wrap, we make a tasty blue cheese sauce to put inside, but you could just as easily use your favorite ranch dressing. And if you don't like buffalo-style sauce, you can use barbecue sauce or even teriyaki sauce for a different twist.

1 lb/455 g boneless, skinless chicken breasts (2 or 3)

2 tbsp butter, melted

¼ cup/60 ml hot sauce

½ cup/55 g crumbled blue cheese

¼ cup/60 ml mayonnaise

¼ cup/60 ml sour cream

Four 10-in/25-cm flour tortillas

1 large tomato

2 cups/55 g shredded iceberg lettuce

Preheat the oven to 350°F/180°C/gas mark 4.

Put the chicken breasts between two sheets of plastic wrap/cling film and gently pound them flat with a meat mallet or the underside of a heavy pot until the pieces are about ¼ in/6 mm thick. Put the chicken in a baking dish. Combine the butter and hot sauce in a small bowl and pour half of the sauce over the chicken. Bake for 15 minutes, or until cooked through. Cut the chicken into strips 1 in/2.5 cm wide.

Meanwhile, combine the cheese, mayonnaise, and sour cream in a small bowl to make buffalo sauce. Lay the tortillas on a flat work surface and spread the blue cheese mixture down the center of each one. Cut the tomato into eight slices. Lay two tomato slices over the blue cheese on each tortilla and top with the shredded lettuce. Dip the chicken strips in the remaining buffalo sauce and arrange them over the lettuce. Fold in the bottom and top of the tortilla and then fold the sides over to form the wrap. Cut in half and serve immediately or wrap individually in plastic wrap/cling film, refrigerate, and serve cold.

GRILLED CHICKEN, TOMATO, AND SPINACH PANINI WITH GAZPACHO SALAD

Jill I had something similar to this at a restaurant on campus one day, and I was shocked at how good it was, mostly because finding good food on a college campus is like the never-ending search for the Holy Grail: No one is quite sure that it even exists. There are several steps to it, so it takes a bit of time to make, but it's definitely worth it.

SALAD

3 Roma tomatoes

1 cucumber

1 red bell pepper/capsicum

½ cup/55 g finely chopped red onion

2 cloves garlic, peeled and finely chopped

2 tbsp fresh lemon juice

2 tbsp olive oil

Salt and pepper

PANINI

4 Roma tomatoes

Olive oil for brushing

4 small boneless, skinless chicken breasts (about 1 lb/455 g)

¼ cup/55 g butter

3 cloves garlic, peeled and finely chopped

6 oz/170 g fresh spinach

8 pieces crusty bread

8 slices provolone or mozzarella cheese

To prepare the salad: Halve and seed the 3 tomatoes. Cut the halves into pieces ½ in/12 mm long and place them in a bowl. Peel the cucumber, cut it into pieces ½ in/12 mm long, and add them to the bowl. Halve, seed, and chop the red bell peppers/capsicums into pieces ¼ in/6mm long, and add them to the bowl. Add the onion and garlic to the bowl.

Put the lemon juice and the 2 tbsp olive oil in a small bowl and stir vigorously to combine. Pour the vinaigrette into the bowl of vegetables and stir until combined. Season with salt and pepper and refrigerate until ready to serve.

To prepare the panini: Preheat a grill/barbecue or grill pan on medium-high heat.

Halve and seed the 4 tomatoes. Brush the tomato halves with olive oil. Grill/barbecue them over high heat for 2 minutes on each side, or until soft.

Grill the chicken for 5 minutes on each side, or until cooked through.

Meanwhile, melt 2 tbsp of the butter in a frying pan over medium heat. Add the chopped garlic and cook, stirring frequently, for 1 minute. Add the spinach and cook for 5 minutes, or until soft.

Spread one side of each piece of bread with the remaining 2 tbsp of butter. Put 4 of the bread slices on a work surface, buttered-sides down. Place 1 slice of cheese on each piece of bread and top with a chicken breast. Place some of the spinach on top of the chicken and top with 2 grilled tomato halves. Place another slice of cheese over the tomatoes and top with the remaining bread slices, buttered-sides up. Place the sandwiches on the grill/barbecue or grill pan and weigh down with a heavy pan or a baking pan with a heavy bowl or pan inside it. Cook the sandwiches for 3 minutes on each side, or until the bread is golden brown and toasted. Slice the sandwiches in half and serve immediately with the gazpacho salad on the side.

Ingredient Info

Extra-virgin olive oil comes from the first press of olives. It is the highest quality with the best color, aroma, and flavor. "Pure" or "virgin" olive oils come from the second press and are less flavorful. Products marked "light" olive oil are lighter in flavor and color but not in calories. In our recipes, we call for just "olive oil." Extra-virgin olive oil would be our first choice, but if it's out of your budget, use one of the others. Your food will taste fine, and the world will not come to an end.

UPSIDE-DOWN CHICKEN POT PIE

Jill

This version of the classic chicken pot pie actually takes less time than usual because you can cook the puff pastry at the same time as the filling. Also, the thyme in this version gives it just enough flavor without being overwhelming. If you're planning on reheating this, you may want to put in a little bit less because the flavor gets stronger over time.

1 small onion

1 carrot

1 russet potato

1 lb/455 g boneless, skinless chicken

4 cups/960 ml Basic Chicken Broth (page 89)

½ cup/60 g frozen peas

¼ tsp dried thyme

Salt and pepper

3 tbsp cornstarch/cornflour

Cooking spray

One 9-in/23-cm sheet puff pastry, thawed

Preheat the oven to 400°F/200°C/gas mark 6.

Peel the onion, carrot, and potato and cut them into pieces ½ in/12 mm long. Cut the chicken into bite-size pieces.

Put the broth, onion, carrot, potato, and chicken in a large saucepan and bring them to a boil. Cook over medium heat for 15 minutes, or until the potato is soft. Add the peas and thyme to the pan, season with salt and pepper, and cook for 5 minutes.

Whisk together the cornstarch/cornflour and ¼ cup/60 ml water in a small bowl until smooth. Pour the mixture into the pan, stirring constantly, and cook for 2 minutes, or until the mixture starts to bubble.

Meanwhile, coat a baking sheet/tray with cooking spray or oil. Cut the puff pastry sheet into quarters and place the pieces on the baking sheet, making sure the pieces aren't touching. Bake for 20 minutes, or until golden brown.

Place a piece of puff pastry on each plate and top with some of the chicken mixture. Serve immediately.

BLACKENED CHICKEN NACHOS WITH GUACAMOLE

Megan

This recipe is inspired by a restaurant in Tempe, Arizona, that makes the most impressive plate of nachos any of our friends has ever seen. Although it isn't something you will eat every day, it is the perfect recipe for entertaining a crowd, and I promise no one will complain. They can also be served with black beans cooked with garlic, onion, and cilantro/fresh coriander for another tasty variation.

CHICKEN NACHOS

1 tsp Cajun seasoning

1 lb/455 g boneless, skinless chicken breasts (2 or 3)

2 large tomatoes

One 13-oz/370-g bag tortilla chips

One 7-oz/200-g can pickled jalapeño slices

4 cups/455 g shredded Cheddar or Jack cheese

GUACAMOLE

1 ripe avocado

2 cloves garlic

Juice of 1 lime

Salt and pepper

1 small tomato

1 tbsp chopped cilantro/ fresh coriander

Salsa, for garnish

Sour cream, for garnish

To prepare the chicken nachos: Preheat the oven to 350°F/ 180°C/gas mark 4.

Put the Cajun seasoning on a plate and dredge (see Lingo, page 78) the chicken breasts in it until completely coated. Heat a nonstick frying pan over high heat and add the chicken. Cook for 1 minute on each side, then put the chicken on a baking sheet/tray. Bake the chicken for 20 minutes, or until cooked through. Remove from the oven and let it rest for 5 minutes. Cut the chicken into cubes ½ in/12 mm long and set aside.

Halve, seed, and cut the large tomatoes into pieces ¼ in/ 6 mm long.

Spread out half of the tortilla chips on a large baking dish. Sprinkle half of the chicken, tomatoes, and jalapeños over the chips and cover with half of the cheese. Make a second layer of chips and top with the remaining chicken, tomatoes, jalapeños, and cheese. Put the dish in the oven and bake for 15 minutes, or until the cheese is melted.

To prepare the guacamole: Cut the avocado in half and remove the pit. Scoop the avocado into a bowl and smash it with a fork. Peel and finely chop the garlic and add it to the bowl. Add the lime juice and season with salt and pepper. Halve, seed, and cut the small tomato into pieces ¼ in/6mm long. Add the small tomato and cilantro/fresh coriander to the bowl and stir until combined.

Serve the nachos with the guacamole, salsa, and sour cream on the side.

CHICKEN TACOS

Jill

I made this recipe for tacos after staring into the pantry trying to decide what to do for dinner. I was shocked at how good they tasted and have been making them ever since. This is a good opportunity to try out different types of spices and figure out what you like. If you like your tacos really spicy, add more red pepper flakes, or try cayenne pepper or hot sauce. You can adjust more or less of any of the spices in the recipe or try adding some different spices, like Cajun seasoning or garlic salt. You can also try adding jalapeños (canned or fresh), extra green chiles, or fresh garlic or tomatoes.

1 lb/455 g boneless, skinless chicken breasts (2 or 3)

1 onion

1 tbsp canola oil

1 tsp garlic powder

½ tsp ground cumin

½ tsp chili powder

Dash of red pepper flakes

One 15-oz/430-g can diced tomatoes, juice reserved

One 4-oz/115-g can diced green chiles, juice reserved

Eight 6-in/15-cm flour tortillas

1½ cups/170 g shredded Cheddar or Jack cheese

Cut the chicken into pieces ½ in/12 mm long. Peel the onion and chop it into pieces ¼ in/6 mm long.

Put the canola oil in a frying pan over medium-high heat. Add the onion and cook for 5 minutes. Add the chicken and cook, stirring often, for 5 minutes more. Add the garlic powder, cumin, chili powder, and red pepper flakes and stir until combined. Add the tomatoes and chiles and their juices and simmer over medium heat for 5 minutes, or until the mixture is thick and saucy.

Spoon some of the chicken onto each tortilla and top with some of the shredded cheese. Serve immediately.

CHICKEN SALTIMBOCCA WITH POTATO GNOCCHI

Megan

Saltimbocca is a traditional southern Italian dish whose name literally means "jump in mouth," which is exactly what happened to our former roommate, Kevin, when he ate an entire family-sized portion. I make homemade gnocchi for this dish, partly because I love it and partly to show you how easy it is. If you're short on time, you can buy fresh gnocchi at most grocery stores.

POTATO GNOCCHI

1 lb/455 g russet potatoes (2 or 3)

1 egg yolk

½ tsp salt

¾ cup/85 g flour

CHICKEN SALTIMBOCCA

4 boneless, skinless chicken breasts
(1 to 1½ lb/455 to 680 g)

12 fresh sage leaves

4 slices prosciutto

¼ cup/30 g flour

Salt and pepper

1 tbsp olive oil

1 tbsp butter

¾ cup/180 ml white wine

¾ cup/180 ml chicken broth

¼ cup/60 ml fresh lemon juice

2 tbsp butter

2 tbsp chopped fresh sage

To prepare the potato gnocchi: Peel the potatoes and cut them into chunks 1 in/2.5 cm wide. Put them in a saucepan of salted water and bring to a boil. Simmer over medium heat for 15 minutes, or until just soft. Drain them well.

Put the potatoes in a large bowl and mash with a potato masher or fork. Add the egg yolk and salt and mix until smooth. Add ½ cup/55 g of the flour and stir until combined. Put the remaining ¼ cup/30 g of the flour on a work surface. Form the dough into a ball and put it on the flour. Roll the ball to cover it with the flour and gently knead the flour into the dough. (Press the ball down with the heel of your hand and then fold it in half.) Continue in this way until all of the flour is incorporated or until the dough is no longer sticky. Split the dough into four pieces and roll each one into a rope ½ in/12 mm in diameter. Cut each rope into pieces 1 in/2.5 cm long.

Bring a large saucepan of salted water to a boil and add the gnocchi. Cook for 2 to 3 minutes, or until they float to the top of the pan. Remove with a slotted spoon and put them on a plate in a single layer. (The gnocchi can be covered and refrigerated for several hours.)

(continued)

To prepare the chicken saltimbocca: Put the chicken breasts between two pieces of plastic wrap/cling film and gently pound them flat with a meat mallet or heavy pot until the pieces are about ¼ in/6 mm thick. Place 3 sage leaves on each chicken breast and top with a slice of prosciutto. Put the flour in a shallow bowl and season with salt and pepper. Dredge (see Lingo, page 78) the chicken in the flour, shaking off the excess.

Heat the olive oil and butter in a large frying pan over medium heat. Put the chicken in the pan, prosciutto-side down. Cook for 3 minutes, or until crisp. Turn over the chicken and cook for 5 minutes more, or until cooked through. Remove the chicken from the pan and cover to keep warm.

Add the wine to the pan, gently scraping the bottom to remove any bits of chicken. Cook for 2 minutes, add the broth and lemon juice, and season with salt and pepper. Cook for 2 minutes more, or until it begins to bubble.

Just prior to serving, melt the 2 tbsp butter in a large frying pan over medium-high heat and add the sage. Add the gnocchi and cook, stirring occasionally, for 5 minutes, or until golden brown.

Place a chicken breast on each plate and top with some of the sauce. Spoon some of the gnocchi next to the chicken and serve immediately.

CHICKEN CURRY

Megan

I really like Indian food, but somehow it never tastes as good at home as when you eat out. So, I was surprised when my boyfriend made me this fast and easy curry that is so tasty. This has become part of our regular repertoire of quick meals to make when we're short on time.

1 lb/455 g boneless, skinless chicken breasts (2 or 3)

1 onion

½ head cauliflower

1 cup/215 g dry white rice

2¼ cups/540 ml water

2 tbsp canola oil

2 tbsp curry powder

2 tbsp flour

3 tbsp tomato paste/puree

1½ cups/360 ml chicken broth

1 cup/120 g frozen peas

½ cup/120 ml plain yogurt

¼ cup/10 g chopped cilantro/ fresh coriander

Cut the chicken into pieces 1½ in/4 cm long. Peel the onion and chop it into pieces ½ in/12 mm long. Remove the florets from the cauliflower and cut any large ones in half.

Put the rice and water in a small saucepan and bring to a boil. Cover and cook over low heat for 20 minutes, or until the rice is tender. Keep warm.

Meanwhile, heat the canola oil in a large frying pan over medium-high heat. Add the onion and cook for 3 minutes. Add the chicken and cook, stirring frequently, for 5 minutes, or until the outside of the chicken is cooked. Add the curry powder and flour and stir until the flour has been absorbed. Add the tomato paste/puree and slowly stir in the broth. Add the cauliflower, cover, and simmer over low heat for 10 minutes. Add the peas and cook for 5 minutes more, or just until the peas are heated through. Remove from the heat and stir in the yogurt.

Spoon some of the rice on each plate and top with the curry. Sprinkle with the cilantro/fresh coriander and serve immediately.

Ingredient Info

Curry powder is actually a blend of many spices and can be found in infinite varieties. Every curry powder has a different blend of different amounts of spices, which makes each one truly unique. Most Indian curry powders you find in the United States are yellow and made up of a combination of coriander, cumin, fenugreek, mustard, chile, and black pepper. Curry powder in India is much more diverse and can be yellow, red, or brown and can contain as many as twenty different spices, including allspice, white pepper, ground mustard, ground ginger, cinnamon, roasted cumin, cloves, nutmeg, mace, cardamom, bay leaves, and coriander seeds.

Asian cultures also have curries, which are typically named for their color. Instead of being used in powder form, they are generally a paste made up of a mixture of fresh ingredients. The most common Asian curries are red curry and green curry. Both are made up of a combination of garlic, shallots, either green or red chiles, galangal, shrimp/prawn paste, kaffir lime peel, cilantro/coriander, and lemon grass. They are most commonly prepared with coconut milk to make a slightly sweet and spicy sauce.

CRISPY TERIYAKI CHICKEN WITH RICE

SERVES 4

Jill

I love this stuff. There's nothing particularly earth-shattering that goes into it, but the combination is delicious. The nice part about stir-fries like this one is that they can easily be adjusted for any number of people. You can double it (if you have a big enough pan) or cut it in half for just two people. And, this is one of the few stir-fries that can be reheated without suffering too much.

1 cup/215 g dry white rice

2¼ cups/540 ml water

1 lb/455 g boneless, skinless chicken breasts (2 or 3)

8 oz/225 g fresh mushrooms

1 head baby bok choy

1 red bell pepper/capsicum

1 onion

1 cup/70 g pea pods

½ cup/120 ml teriyaki sauce

¼ cup/60 ml soy sauce

1 tsp grated peeled fresh ginger

Canola oil for frying

½ cup/55 g cornstarch/cornflour

Put the rice and water in a small saucepan and bring them to a boil. Cover and cook over low heat for 20 minutes, or until the rice is tender. Keep warm.

Cut the chicken into cubes 1 in/2.5 cm wide. Remove the stem ends from the mushrooms and thinly slice the caps. Cut the bok choy into slices ¼ in/6 mm thick. Halve, seed, and cut the red bell pepper/capsicum into slices ¼ in/6 mm thick. Peel the onion and cut it into slices ¼ in/6 mm thick. Remove the stems and strings from the pea pods (see Ingredients Info, page 26).

Combine the teriyaki sauce, soy sauce, and ginger in a small bowl and set aside.

Heat about ½ in/1.25 cm of the canola oil in a large frying pan over medium-high heat. Toss the chicken in the cornstarch/cornflour and cook it in the oil for 2 minutes on each side, or until cooked through. Remove the chicken to paper towels/absorbent paper to drain.

Drain the oil from the pan, leaving just enough to coat the bottom. Add the mushrooms, bok choy, red bell pepper/capsicum, and onion and cook for 10 minutes, or until the vegetables are slightly soft. Add the pea pods and cook for 3 minutes, or until they brighten in color. Add the teriyaki mixture and cook for 1 minute, or until warm. Stir in the cooked chicken and serve immediately over the rice.

Ingredient Info

Here is a question that plagued me for years: How do you measure pea pods? If you put them in a measuring cup, they stick out all over. So do you try to adjust for the amount that's sticking out by filling the cup a little looser? Or do you smash them all down in the cup, breaking them apart in the process? Unfortunately, I don't know the answer, so I stopped trying to measure them. We give you measurements so you have an idea how many to put in, but they usually just get used in stir-fry, so how much can it really matter? If it says 1 cup, grab a handful. If it says 1½ cups, grab a big handful. That's close enough.

GARLIC CHICKEN WITH SWISS CHARD SERVES 4

Jill

This is another recipe I swiped from my friend Jess's mom. I've had it several times when I've been there, and I love the creamy garlic flavor. I'm not sure if it's an old family recipe, but it took me months and months to get it out of her. I finally wore her down, and I am eternally grateful . . . and you will be, too.

4 boneless, skinless chicken breasts
(1 to 1½ lb/450 to 680g)

1 tsp garlic salt

1 cup/115 g dry bread crumbs

1 egg

2 tbsp canola oil

4 cloves garlic

¼ cup/55 g butter

¼ cup/30 g flour

4 cups/960 ml chicken broth

3 tbsp fresh lemon juice

Salt and pepper

12 oz/340 g Swiss chard

Preheat the oven to 325°F/165°C/gas mark 3.

Pat the chicken dry with a paper towel/absorbent paper and season both sides with the garlic salt. Put the bread crumbs in a shallow bowl. Beat the egg in a shallow bowl with 1 tbsp water. Heat the canola oil in a large frying pan over medium-high heat. Dip the chicken breasts in the egg mixture and then in the bread crumbs, and put them in the pan. Cook for 3 to 4 minutes on each side, or until golden brown. Put the chicken breasts in a baking pan and set aside.

Peel and finely chop the garlic. Wipe any bread crumbs from the pan, add the butter, and melt over medium-high heat. Add the garlic and cook, stirring constantly, for 1 minute. Stir in the flour and cook for 1 minute. Slowly add the broth, stirring until completely smooth. Add the lemon juice and cook, stirring frequently, for 3 minutes, or until the sauce has thickened. Season with salt and pepper and pour over the chicken breasts. Bake for 30 to 40 minutes, or until the chicken is cooked through.

Meanwhile, cut any large stems from the chard and roughly chop the leaves. Put enough water in a large frying pan to barely cover the bottom. Bring it to a simmer over medium heat and add the chard. Cook, stirring occasionally, for 10 minutes, or until completely soft. Drain the chard and keep warm.

Place a chicken breast and some of the chard on each plate. Spoon the sauce over the chicken and chard and serve immediately.

> ## On a Budget

I was throwing away part of a dried-out loaf of French bread when it dawned on me that I was going to get rid of the bread and then go buy bread crumbs—not my smartest move. Now I throw the dried bread in the blender or food processor and pulse it until it is fairly fine. Then I put a strainer over a bowl and dump in the crumbs. The ones that fall through to the bowl I use as regular bread crumbs, and the ones that stay in the sieve I use instead of buying coarser panko bread crumbs. Store them separately in resealable bags, and you'll always have them when you need them.

ROASTED CHICKEN
WITH ROASTED THYME POTATOES

Megan

This is one of my favorite Sunday lunch meals. There is nothing better than sitting home on a lazy Sunday with the delicious smell of roasting garlic and lime floating through the house. Instead of roasted potatoes, I often serve this with a special version of Spanish rice with red and green bell pepper/capsicum added to it for a Megan version of something Mexicanesque.

CHICKEN

**1 whole chicken (4 to 5 lb/
1.8 to 2.3 kg)**

**One ²/₃-oz/20-g package fresh thyme
(3 tbsp leaves reserved)**

1 clove garlic

¼ cup/60 ml fresh lime juice

2 tbsp honey

1 tbsp olive oil

Salt and pepper

POTATOES

2 lb/910 g small red potatoes (6 or 7)

2 tbsp olive oil

Salt and pepper

**5 tsp minced fresh thyme (from the
leaves reserved above)**

To prepare the chicken: Preheat the oven to 350°F/180°C/ gas mark 4.

Rinse the chicken under cold water and discard any parts from the cavity. Put the chicken in a roasting pan/tray and pat dry with a paper towel/absorbent paper.

Put the fresh thyme inside the cavity of the chicken. Loosely tie the legs of the chicken together with kitchen string right above the knobby ends of the leg. (This helps the chicken cook evenly.)

Peel and finely chop the ' the reserved thyme leaves, the lime jı oil in a small bowl and stir until com nixture over the chicken and seasor epper. Roast the chicken, brushing ν y 20 minutes. Cook for 60 to 75 min the thigh run clear when poked with ature reaches 160°F/70°C.

To prepare the pota .f and put them on a baking sheet/tra,. _, ı over the pota- toes and toss until completely coated. Sprinkle with the minced thyme. Bake for 30 minutes, or until golden brown and tender.

Remove the thyme stems from the chicken cavity and place the chicken on a large serving plate. Spoon the potatoes around it and serve immediately.

Cooking Tip

If you only need 1 or 2 tbsp of thyme leaves, look for the biggest stems, pull off any small stems, then wrap your fingers around the stem and pull gently to remove the leaves. If you need more than that, get out the scissors and start snipping the leaves off the stems.

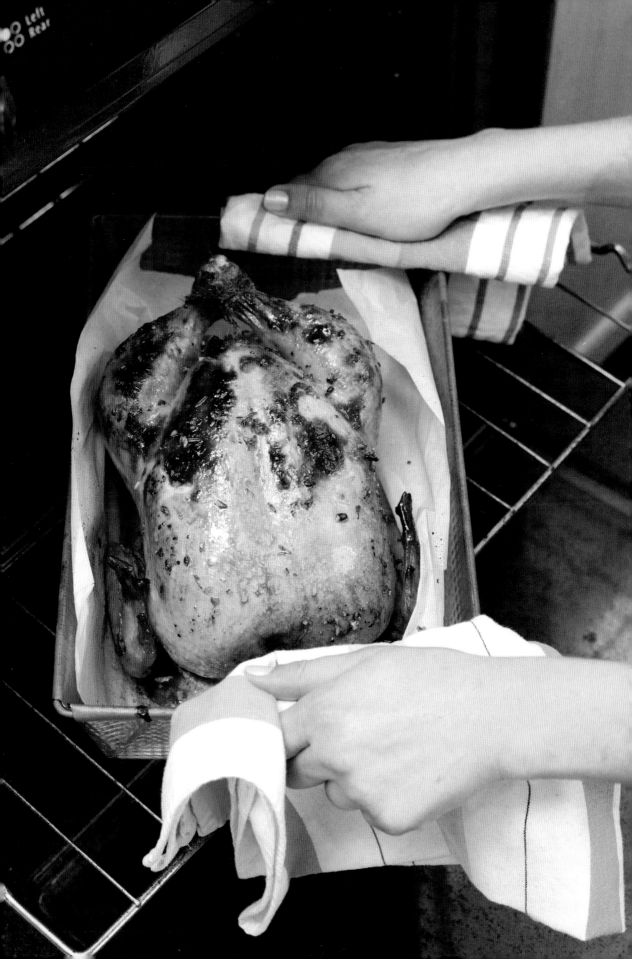

Chapter

5

BEEF

There are two basic ways to cook meat: moist heat, which is low and slow, or dry heat, which is high and hot. Which method you use depends on the cut of meat. Tougher or fattier cuts of meat need longer cooking times and benefit from cooking in liquid, which is called braising or stewing. Leaner, more tender cuts of meat are best when cooked quickly over high heat as in grilling, roasting, or broiling. The key is to understand which category different cuts fall into so you can make appropriate choices.

Any cuts of beef that have "chuck" in the name, such as **chuck roast**, **chuck steak**, **chuck cross-rib roast**, **chuck shoulder roast**, **chuck blade steak**, or **chuck 7-bone roast,** and anything labeled as **pot roast** are basically the same thing. What they are called depends on the butcher, the region, how it was cut, and where exactly it came from on the steer. The technicalities don't really matter to you. All you need to know is that for your purposes they are interchangeable and they all require longer cooking times. Some of these cuts have bones and some don't. It doesn't matter which you buy unless you specifically want the bones for making stock. These meats are very flavorful and are perfect for pot roast, soups, and stews.

Brisket is another cut that needs the moisture and low heat of braising but is delicious just sliced or shredded for barbecued beef.

Skirt steaks, flank steak, rib-eye, sirloin, T-bone, Porterhouse, New York strip, and **filet** are more tender cuts of meat that are good for grilling or broiling. Sirloin, which is our first choice for dishes such as stir-fries or stroganoff, is generally the least expensive of this group. **Round steak** also falls in this category, but it's tough and dry, and we've never found a good way to cook it.

Rib roast, tenderloin, rump roast, top round roast, and **bottom round roast** are all good for roasting. Rib roasts, also called prime rib (which is what rib-eyes are cut from) and tenderloin (which is what filets are cut from), are the most tender of these roasts but also the most expensive.

BEEF USES

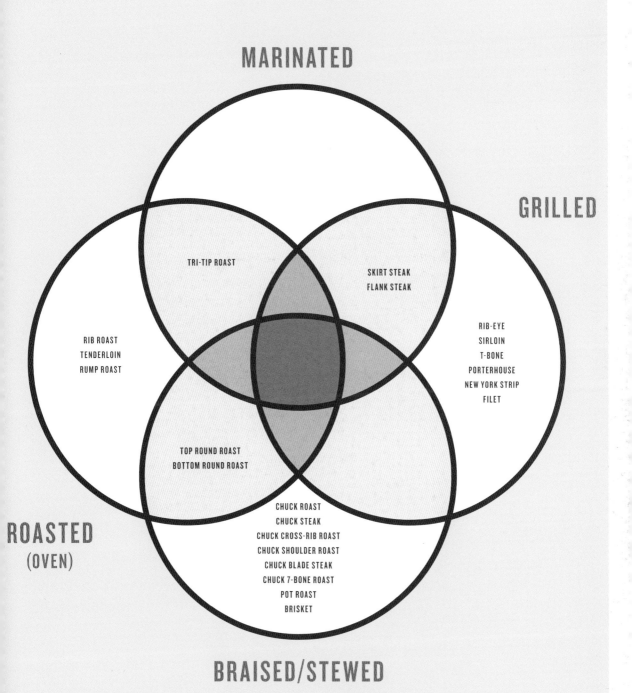

MARINATED

GRILLED

ROASTED
(OVEN)

BRAISED/STEWED

TRI-TIP ROAST

SKIRT STEAK
FLANK STEAK

RIB ROAST
TENDERLOIN
RUMP ROAST

RIB-EYE
SIRLOIN
T-BONE
PORTERHOUSE
NEW YORK STRIP
FILET

TOP ROUND ROAST
BOTTOM ROUND ROAST

CHUCK ROAST
CHUCK STEAK
CHUCK CROSS-RIB ROAST
CHUCK SHOULDER ROAST
CHUCK BLADE STEAK
CHUCK 7-BONE ROAST
POT ROAST
BRISKET

BEEF STROGANOFF

Jill

I could eat this every night. That sounds like an exaggeration, but I really never get sick of it. Every night when we argue about what to eat for dinner, I suggest this, and my boyfriend gives me that look and suggests something else. It's also our sister Mindy's all-time favorite food. Whenever she has a really bad day, she calls my mom and asks her to make it for dinner. Yep. It's that good.

12 oz/340 g dry egg noodles

1 lb/455 g sirloin steak

8 oz/225 g fresh mushrooms

1 large onion

1 tbsp canola oil

2 tbsp cornstarch/cornflour

One 14-oz/400-g can beef broth

Salt and pepper

½ cup/120 ml sour cream

Bring a large saucepan of salted water to a boil. Add the noodles and cook, stirring occasionally, for 10 minutes, or until al dente. Drain and keep warm.

Cut the sirloin into thin slices about 2 in/5 cm long. Remove the stem ends from the mushrooms and slice the caps. Peel, halve, and cut the onion into slices ¼ in/6 mm thick.

Put the canola oil in a large frying pan over medium-high heat. Add the mushrooms and onion and cook for 10 minutes, or until the onion is soft. Push the onion and mushrooms to the side of the pan and add the meat. Cook, stirring frequently for 5 minutes, or until the meat is completely browned. Combine the cornstarch/cornflour with enough of the broth to create a smooth, pourable slurry (see Cooking Tip, page 94). Pour the remaining broth into the pan and bring it to a boil. Stir in the slurry and cook, stirring constantly for 1 minute, or until the sauce is bubbly and thick. Season with salt and pepper, remove from the heat, and stir in the sour cream. Serve immediately over the noodles.

Ingredient Info

Mushrooms should never be soaked in water. They are like little sponges and can easily become waterlogged. Brush them off with a soft brush (a soft toothbrush works well), briefly put them under running water, and pat them dry.

BEEF BOURGUIGNON

Megan

After seeing the recent movie about Julia Child *(Julie & Julia),* I was inspired to try her famous recipe for beef bourguignon. And I did. Once. It was delicious, but do you have any idea how long it takes to peel a pound/half kilogram of pearl onions? And that was just one step. I admire people with that type of conviction; unfortunately, I don't have it. So this may not be Julia's version, but it is quite tasty.

8 oz/225 g bacon/streaky bacon

3 lb/1.4 kg chuck roast

Salt and pepper

1 lb/455 g carrots

2 onions

2 cloves garlic

1 tbsp tomato paste/puree

One 14-oz/400-g can beef broth

2 cups/480 ml red wine

½ tsp dried thyme

1 lb/455 g fresh mushrooms

¼ cup/55 g butter

¼ cup/30 g flour

2 cups/340 g frozen pearl onions

Preheat the oven to 300°F/150°C/gas mark 2.

Cut the bacon into pieces 1 in/2.5 cm long and put them in a large Dutch oven or other heavy ovenproof pot. Cut the chuck roast into pieces 2 in/5 cm long and pat dry with a paper towel/absorbent paper. Cook the bacon over medium heat, stirring occasionally, for 10 minutes, or until lightly browned. Remove the bacon from the pan. Add enough beef to barely cover the bottom of the Dutch oven. Brown the meat on all sides and remove from the pan. Repeat the process with the remaining meat, then season it all with salt and pepper.

Peel the carrots and cut them into pieces 2 in/5 cm long. Peel and halve the onions and then cut each half into quarters. Peel and finely chop the garlic. Put the carrots and onions in the pot over medium heat and cook, stirring occasionally, for 5 minutes, or until lightly browned. Stir in the tomato paste/puree and then slowly stir in the broth. Add the beef, bacon, garlic, wine, and thyme and season with salt and pepper. Bring to a boil, cover tightly, and bake for 2 hours, or until the meat is tender.

Meanwhile, remove the stem ends from the mushrooms and cut the caps in half. Melt 2 tbsp of the butter in a frying pan and add the mushrooms. Cook, stirring occasionally, for 10 minutes, or until browned.

Remove the pot from the oven and put it on the stove over medium heat. Stir together the flour and the remaining 2 tbsp of butter and stir them into the sauce. Season with salt and pepper. Add the mushrooms and pearl onions and cook for 15 minutes, or until the sauce is thickened and the onions are tender. Serve immediately.

BEEF AND GUINNESS PIE

Jill

I fell in love with this dish when I was in Ireland. So, of course, I had to try to make it when I got home. It took a couple of attempts to get it just right, but my boyfriend, Andrew, was happy with every version. As he said, "Meat and Guinness—what could be wrong with that?" I think you'll agree.

2- to 2½-lb/910-g to 1.2-kg boneless chuck roast

2 tbsp canola oil

1 large onion

2 cloves garlic

⅓ cup/40 g flour

2 tbsp tomato paste/puree

1 cup/240 ml beef broth

1 cup/240 ml Guinness stout beer

2 tbsp Worcestershire sauce

Salt and pepper

One 9-in/23-cm sheet puff pastry, thawed

1 egg

Cut the chuck roast into pieces 1 in/2.5 cm long and pat dry with a paper towel/absorbent paper. Heat the canola oil in a large saucepan over medium-high heat and add enough meat to barely cover the bottom of the pan. Brown the meat on all sides and remove it from the pan. Repeat the process with the remaining meat.

Peel, halve, and cut the onion into slices ¼ in/6 mm thick. Add the onion to the empty pan and cook, stirring frequently, for 5 minutes, or until it begins to soften.

Meanwhile, peel and roughly chop the garlic. Add the garlic to the pan and cook, stirring constantly, for 30 seconds. Add the flour and tomato paste/puree and stir until smooth. Add the broth, Guinness, and Worcestershire and stir well. Return the meat to the pan and season with salt and pepper. Bring to a boil, reduce the heat to medium-low, and simmer for 1½ to 2 hours, or until the meat is very tender.

Preheat the oven to 400°F/200°C/gas mark 6.

Spoon the beef mixture into a 2-qt/2-L baking dish. Put the sheet of puff pastry over the top of the dish, being careful not to lay the pastry directly on the meat. (If the pastry sits on the sauce, it will not rise properly.) Press the pastry tightly around the sides of the pan. Beat the egg well and brush it over the pastry. Bake for 20 minutes, or until the pastry is golden brown. Serve immediately.

Cooking Tip

Browning foods serves two purposes: It gives them a richer flavor, and it makes them look more appetizing. Brown meat or vegetables in oil over medium-high to high heat so the outsides sear quickly, sealing the juices inside. Make sure the ingredients are dry before putting them in the pan, though, or the liquid will make them steam rather than sear. If you are browning with a small amount of oil, meat will sometimes stick to the pan. If it does, leave it alone for another minute. Once the meat is seared, it will release from the pan by itself.

GREEN CHILE–CHEESE MEATLOAF
WITH ROASTED BUTTERNUT SQUASH

Megan

If you are anything like me, you hear the word "meatloaf" and automatically think either old-people food or mystery meat from the school cafeteria. The funny thing is, I have always liked meatloaf; my dad's special recipe can't be beat. Plus, meatloaf is just like a hamburger, and who doesn't like hamburgers? How did meatloaf get such a bad rap? I don't have the answer, but maybe this new version of meatloaf, with loads of green chiles and a tasty layer of Cheddar cheese, will change how people think about this standby. I always make this with the roasted squash because they can bake at the same time, but if you aren't a squash fan, feel free to skip it.

MEATLOAF

1 small onion

One 27-oz/765-g can whole green chiles

2 lb/910 g ground/minced beef

1 lb/455 g ground/minced pork

½ cup/55 g dried bread crumbs

2 large eggs

1 tsp ground cumin

1 tsp salt

½ tsp pepper

6 oz/170 g Cheddar cheese

SQUASH

1 large butternut squash (about 2 lb/910 g)

2 tbsp canola oil

Salt and Pepper

To prepare the meatloaf: Preheat the oven to 350°F/180°C/ gas mark 4.

Peel and finely chop the onion. Drain, halve, and seed the green chiles. Pat them dry with a paper towel/absorbent paper, set aside four halves, and cut the remaining chiles into pieces ¼ in/6 mm long.

Put the onion, diced chiles, beef, pork, bread crumbs, eggs, cumin, salt, and pepper in a large bowl and mix with your hands until completely combined. Put half of the meat on a baking sheet/ tray and form the bottom of the meatloaf (about 6 in/15 cm by 10 in/25 cm). Cut the cheese into slices ¼ in/6 mm thick and lay the slices down the center of the meat, leaving about 1 in/2.5 cm open around the edges. Put the remaining meat over the cheese and press firmly around the edges to seal in the cheese. Bake for 75 minutes. Lay the whole chiles on top of the meatloaf and bake for 15 minutes more, or until the meatloaf is cooked through. Let it rest for 10 minutes, then place it on a serving platter and slice.

To prepare the squash: Cut the squash into large chunks, remove the seeds and skin, and then cut it into pieces 1 in/2.5 cm long. (Cutting it into chunks first makes it much easier to peel.) Put the squash on a baking sheet/tray, add the canola oil, and toss until coated. Season with salt and pepper and bake with the meatloaf for 45 minutes, or until tender and browned on the edges.

Place the squash in a serving bowl and serve it with the meatloaf.

ROPA VIEJA

Jill

This recipe comes from my friend Jess's mom, Miriam, who is Cuban. It actually means "old clothes" in Spanish, which sounds pretty unappealing, but don't let that fool you. Every time I go to their house for dinner, I hope this is on the menu because it is so good! It's not spicy at all, but it has a lot of flavor. With twelve cloves of garlic you'd think that it would be overpowering, but it's not. The meat just really sucks up the garlic flavor. This is traditionally served on rice, but it would also be really good with tortillas.

2 lb/910 g flank or skirt steak

12 cloves garlic

Salt and pepper

1 onion

2 green bell peppers/capsicums

3 tbsp canola oil

One 8-oz/225-g can tomato sauce

One 6-oz/170-g can tomato paste/puree

¼ cup/60 ml dry red wine

1 tsp ground cumin

½ tsp dried oregano

2¾ cups/660 ml water

1 cup/215 g dry rice

Put the steak in a large pot and add enough water to cover the meat by 1 in/2.5 cm. Peel 4 of the garlic cloves, add them to the pan, and season the meat with salt and pepper. Bring to a boil, and simmer over medium heat for 1½ hours, or until the meat is tender. Remove the meat from the pan and cool slightly. Tear the meat into thin strips and set aside.

Meanwhile, peel the onion and cut it into pieces ½ in/12 mm thick. Peel and finely chop the remaining 8 cloves of garlic. Halve, seed, and chop the bell peppers/capsicums into pieces ¼ in/6 mm thick.

Heat the canola oil in large saucepan over medium heat, add the onion and bell peppers/capsicums and cook for 10 minutes, or until slightly softened. Add the garlic, and cook for 1 minute. Add the tomato sauce, tomato paste/puree, wine, cumin, oregano, and ½ cup/120 ml of the water and stir well. Season with salt and pepper and cook for 2 minutes. Add the meat and stir until completely coated with the sauce. Cook, stirring occasionally, for 20 minutes.

Put the rice and remaining 2¼ cup/540 ml water in a small saucepan and bring to a boil. Cook over low heat for 20 minutes, or until the rice is tender.

Place some of the rice on each plate and top with the meat. Serve immediately.

MONGOLIAN BEEF

Megan

Stir-fry is never really hard, but this takes the word "easy" to another level. Cut up the meat and put it in a mix of soy sauce and a couple of other ingredients, and you are finished. Oh, wait—you have to slice the green/spring onions in half, too. What a nightmare! I made this along with a couple of other dishes for a night with friends, and this was the hands-down favorite.

1 clove garlic

1 bunch green/spring onions (about 6)

1 lb/455 g flank steak

½ cup/120 ml soy sauce

¼ cup/50 g dark brown sugar

3 small dried whole red chiles

2 tbsp Asian chili paste

1 tbsp finely chopped peeled
fresh ginger

2¾ cups/660 ml water

1 cup/215 g dry white rice

1 tbsp/15 ml canola oil

Peel and finely chop the garlic. Remove the roots and about 1 in/2.5 cm of the dark green end from the onions. Cut the onions in half lengthwise. Slice the steak into thin pieces (⅛ in/3.5 mm is ideal, but slice as thinly as you're able and make sure your slices are of fairly uniform thickness).

Combine the soy sauce, brown sugar, chiles, chili paste, ginger, garlic, and ½ cup/120 ml of the water in a bowl. Put the flank steak in a resealable bag and pour the marinade into the bag. Refrigerate at least 1 hour or overnight.

Put the rice and the remaining 2¼ cups/540 ml water in a small saucepan and bring to a boil. Cover and cook over low heat for 20 minutes, or until the rice is tender. Keep warm.

Heat the canola oil in a large frying pan over high heat. Add the onions and cook for 30 seconds. Add the beef and the marinade and cook, stirring constantly, for 5 minutes, or until the beef is no longer pink.

Place some of the rice on each plate and top with the meat and onions.

On the Lighter Side

You have to love it when something this easy is also low calorie. At about 450 cal, 28 g of protein, and only 12 g of fat (even including the rice!), this dish will be one you make over and over again.

BEEF AND BROCCOLI WITH RICE NOODLES

Jill

This is one of those Chinese food standards that I love, but it always seems just a bit greasy. When I tried this version, I was pretty impressed with myself because it was flavorful without having too much oil. And, serving it with the rice noodles is a nice difference from regular white rice. 525 calories, 32 grams of protein, 10 grams of fat. That pretty much says it all.

12 oz/340 g dry rice noodles
(see below)

1 lb/455 g fresh broccoli

1 lb/455 g sirloin steak

1 tbsp canola oil

2 cloves garlic

2 tbsp oyster sauce

2 tbsp soy sauce

1 tbsp cornstarch/cornflour

Bring a large saucepan of salted water to a boil and add the noodles. Cook, stirring occasionally for 6 minutes, or until soft. Drain and keep warm.

Meanwhile, trim the florets from the broccoli and discard the stems. Put the broccoli in a microwave-safe bowl and add enough water to just cover the bottom. Cover with plastic wrap/cling film and cook on high for 4 minutes, or until tender-crisp. Drain and set aside.

Cut the meat into thin slices about 2 in/5 cm long. Put the canola oil in a large frying pan over medium-high heat and add the meat. Cook, stirring frequently for 5 minutes, or until completely browned. Peel and finely chop the garlic. Add the garlic to the pan and cook, stirring constantly for 1 minute. Whisk together the oyster sauce, soy sauce, cornstarch/cornflour, and 2 tbsp water in a small bowl and add to the pan. Cook, stirring constantly for 2 minutes, or until bubbly. Add the broccoli and noodles and stir until completely coated with the sauce. Serve immediately.

On a Budget

I love the chewy texture of rice noodles, but unless you find them on sale or at an Asian market they can cost twice as much as regular pasta. If the rice noodles stretch your budget, use vermicelli instead. The dish will still taste great, and your wallet will be much happier.

THAI GREEN CURRY BEEF

Megan

If you have ever had Thai food before, you may have noticed that there are three standard ingredients that you will find in just about everything: lime, cilantro/fresh coriander, and the cute little red chiles that look so sweet but will start a five-alarm fire in your mouth if you aren't careful. All of those flavors with the addition of coconut milk—another Thai favorite—come together to make this a fun dish to pull off at home.

1 cup/215 g dry white rice

2¼ cups/540 ml water

1 onion

1 red bell pepper/capsicum

1½ cups/100 g snap peas

2 limes

1 lb/455 g sirloin steak

1 tbsp canola oil

3 tbsp green curry paste (see Ingredient Info, page 107)

1 tbsp finely chopped peeled fresh ginger

One 13-oz/405-ml can coconut milk

3 small dried whole red Thai chiles

¼ cup/10 g chopped cilantro/fresh coriander

Put the rice and water in a small saucepan and bring to a boil. Cover and cook over low heat for 20 minutes, or until the rice is tender. Keep warm.

Peel the onion and cut it into slices ¼ in/6 mm thick. Halve, seed, and cut the bell pepper/capsicum into strips ¼ in/6mm thick. Remove the stems and strings from the pea pods (see Ingredient Info, page 26). Cut 1 lime into wedges for the garnish. Grate the zest from the remaining lime, cut it in half, and juice it. Cut the sirloin into very thin strips.

Heat the canola oil in a large frying pan and add the onion, bell pepper/capsicum, and pea pods. Cook, stirring frequently, for 3 minutes. Add the steak and cook for 5 minutes, stirring frequently, or until the meat is completely browned. Add the curry paste and ginger and cook for 2 minutes. Add the coconut milk and whole chiles and simmer over low heat for 10 minutes, or until the meat is cooked through. Stir in the lime zest and juice and remove from the heat.

Place some of the rice on each plate and top with the curry. Sprinkle with the cilantro/fresh coriander, place a lime wedge on each plate, and serve immediately.

Cooking Tip

Okay, it's time to admit I'm completely rice-challenged. We wrote the directions for making rice the way the manufacturers suggest, but when I make it that way, I always lose track of the time and it ends up stuck to the bottom of the pan. I've given up even trying it that way. Instead of measuring the water, I just put in a lot, cook it as the recipe says, and then drain off the extra water. So, if you are rice-challenged like me, try it this way. It turns out perfectly, and you don't have to spend all that time trying to scrub the cooked-on rice off the bottom of the pan.

HORSERADISH-CRUSTED STEAK
WITH HORSERADISH MASHED POTATOES

Megan

Prepared horseradish is one of my favorite condiments, and it's even more popular in Austria and Germany. They serve freshly grated horseradish as a complement to lamb, beef, and even hot dogs (which they eat with their hands and no bun). Anyway, this horseradish crust adds a nice sharpness to the steak. And the horseradish mashed potatoes are so good that, once you've tried them, you'll want to serve them with everything.

MASHED POTATOES

2 lb/910 g russet potatoes (4 or 5)

¼ cup/55 g butter

½ cup/120 ml milk

2 tbsp/30 ml prepared horseradish

Salt and pepper

STEAK

¼ cup/55 g butter

1 cup/115 g dry bread crumbs

2 tbsp chopped fresh parsley

2 tbsp/30 ml prepared horseradish

4 thick-cut filet or sirloin steaks (about 2 lb/910 g)

To prepare the mashed potatoes: Peel the potatoes, cut them into chunks, and put them in a large saucepan of salted water. Cook over medium heat for 20 minutes, or until soft. Drain off the water and return the pan to the stove. Add the butter and the milk to the pan and cook over medium heat until the milk comes to a boil. Smash the potatoes with a fork or potato masher until fairly smooth, stir in the horseradish, and season with salt and pepper. Keep warm.

To prepare the steak: Melt the butter. Put the bread crumbs, butter, parsley, and horseradish in a bowl and stir until combined.

Preheat a grill/barbecue or grill pan on high heat and preheat the broiler.

Grill/barbecue the steaks for 3 to 5 minutes on each side, or until the desired doneness (see Cooking Tip, below, taking into account you will be finishing under the broiler). Put the steaks in a baking dish and top them evenly with the bread crumb mixture. Pat the bread crumbs into a smooth layer that covers the entire steak. Put the steaks under the broiler for 5 minutes, or until the topping is browned.

Serve the steaks immediately with a side of mashed potatoes.

> ## Cooking Tip
>
> Knowing when steaks are done can be a challenge to even the most experienced cooks. The most accurate way is to use a meat thermometer. A rare steak is 125°F/52°C; medium-rare 130° to 135°F/54° to 57°C; medium 140° to 145°F/60° to 63°C; medium-well 150° to 155°F/ 66° to 68°C; and well-done is 160°F/71°C. If you don't have a thermometer or just like to live dangerously, you can test the temperature by touch. When you press a rare steak in the center, it feels soft and squishy; medium-rare yields gently to the touch; medium only yields slightly to the touch; medium-well is firm to the touch; and well-done is hard to the touch. If both of those methods seem like too much trouble, stick a knife in the center and look at the amount of pinkness.

130

POT ROAST

I am the queen of comfort food. I like a lot of different types of food, but there's nothing like a classic pot roast. This pot roast is nice and tender, with a really good flavor. Don't skip browning the meat before putting it in the oven though. It makes a huge difference in the flavor.

4 carrots

2 stalks celery

2 onions

2 russet potatoes

2- to 2½-lb/910-g to 1.2-kg chuck roast

2 tbsp canola oil

Salt and pepper

2 tbsp flour

One 14-oz/400-g can beef broth

Preheat the oven to 350°F/180°C/gas mark 4.

Peel the carrots and cut them and the celery into pieces 2 in/5 cm long. Peel and halve the onions and then cut each half in quarters. Peel the potatoes and cut them into chunks 2 in/5 cm long.

Cut the chuck roast into chunks 2 in/5 cm long, removing any large pieces of fat. Heat the canola oil in a frying pan over medium-high heat. Pat the meat dry with a paper towel/absorbent paper and add to the pan. Cook the meat for 5 minutes, or until browned on all sides. Remove the meat from the pan and put it in a baking dish. Season generously with salt and pepper. Stir the flour into the pan. Slowly add the broth, scraping up any bits of meat, and stir until smooth. Pour the broth over the meat. Arrange the carrots, celery, onions, and potatoes around the meat and cover the pan tightly with aluminum foil. Bake for 2 to 2½ hours, or until the meat is very tender. Remove it from the oven and serve immediately.

133

Lingo

Deglazing is one of those terms that can make you say, "Huh?" It simply means to add liquid to a hot pan where food has been cooked in order to release the food particles that are stuck to the pan. Those bits of meat or vegetables, which are called the "fond," are loaded with flavor, and deglazing releases that into the liquid. So if you want to impress someone with your cooking savvy, just say, "I'm deglazing the pan to release the fond."

ROAST BEEF WITH
ROASTED PARSLEY POTATOES

Megan I never realized how many people are afraid of a little pink in their meat! I worked at a steak house for a while, and I was always sad when people would ruin a perfectly good steak or prime rib by ordering it well-done and then dousing it with steak sauce. When you cook beef until it's well-done, you lose all of the delicious juiciness and flavor of the meat. I think roast beef should be eaten rare or medium-rare. Now, I don't want to preach . . . Okay, who am I kidding? Of course I want to preach. But if you normally eat your meat well-done, swing out and try this recipe medium or medium-well. Maybe you will discover there is something to a little pink.

ROAST BEEF

3 lb/1.4 kg sirloin tip or rump roast

Salt and pepper

POTATOES

3 lb/1.4 kg small red potatoes (about 12)

3 tbsp butter, melted

Salt and pepper

¼ cup/10 g chopped fresh parsley

To prepare the roast beef: Preheat the oven to 350°F/180°C/ gas mark 4.

Season the entire roast with salt and a generous amount of pepper. Put the roast in a baking pan/tray and cook for 1 hour and 15 minutes, or until it reaches the desired doneness. (See Cooking Tips, below.) Let it rest for 15 minutes, slice it thinly, and place the slices on a serving platter.

To prepare the potatoes: Cut the potatoes in half and put them on a baking sheet/tray. Drizzle with the melted butter and toss until completely coated. Season with salt and pepper and bake for 40 minutes, or until golden brown and tender. Place the potatoes in a serving bowl, add the parsley, and stir until evenly coated.

Serve immediately.

Cooking Tip

A rough rule of thumb for cooking beef roasts is that it takes about 25 minutes per 1 lb/455 g for rare, 28 minutes for medium, and 30 for well-done. Because these times vary depending on the thickness of the roast, the only way to be sure is by using a meat thermometer. Rare meat will measure 140°F/60°C; medium will be 160°F/71°C; and well-done will be 170°F/77°C. Beef roasts need to rest for 15 minutes after being removed from the oven, though, and during that time they will continue to cook, so remove the roast when it is 10 degrees less than the final temperature you want.

CHILI

Megan

My time in Arizona has made me realize that chili is nowhere near as simple and straightforward as I thought. You can make it with green chiles, with ground/minced beef, with chunks of beef, with pork, with beans, without beans, with chicken—even white chili, and the list could go on. This is my mom's chili, which was the only one I knew growing up, and, while my family is very far from having any Mexican roots, I still think hers is one of the best. You certainly can't call it traditional or authentic, but it is delicious and is still a requirement on Christmas tree–decorating day in the Carle house!

1 onion

1½ lb/680 g ground/minced beef

One 15-oz/430-g can kidney beans, liquid reserved

Three 15-oz/430-g cans diced tomatoes, juices reserved

¼ cup/30 g chili powder

Salt and pepper

3 cups/700 ml water

8 oz/225 g dry macaroni

Peel the onion and cut it into slices ¼ to ½ in/6 to 12 mm wide. Put the beef and onion in a large sauce pot and cook over medium-high heat for 10 minutes, or until the meat is cooked through.

Drain off any fat and add the kidney beans with their liquid, tomatoes and their juice, and chili powder. Bring to a boil and cook over medium-low heat for 15 minutes. Season with salt and pepper and additional chili powder, if desired. Add 3 cups/720 ml water to the pan and bring it to a boil. Stir in the macaroni and cook for 15 minutes, or until the macaroni is al dente. Serve immediately.

On the Lighter Side

I'll admit I never thought of chili as a low-calorie food. When I looked at the ingredients for this dish, I started to wonder, so I ran it through our nutrition software. I was amazed to find that if you use 93 percent lean ground/minced beef, this dish comes in at only 515 calories for 2 cups. I think I need to start eating more chili.

Chapter 6

PORK

Like beef, pork can be cooked either low and slow or high and hot. Fattier cuts of meat need the longer cooking times and moisture of braising or stewing. Leaner cuts of meat are better when grilled, broiled, or roasted over high heat. Many people like their pork thoroughly cooked (not at all pink in the center), which is easy when you are braising or stewing, but when grilling or roasting it can be a little trickier. It's hard to tell from the outside how done the inside is, and overcooked meat will be dry. This is where a meat thermometer comes in handy. Thermometers are inexpensive and keep you from having to repeatedly cut into a roast or chop to see if the middle is done. Simply cook the meat to 160°F/71°C for well-done pork and to 150°F/65°C for slightly pink meat and it will be juicy and safe to eat.

Pork roasts that have "picnic" or "shoulder" in the name—such as **picnic roast, shoulder picnic roast,** or **shoulder arm roast**—need slow cooking. Some have bones and some don't, but it doesn't change the cooking time or method. These roasts are perfect for carnitas or pulled pork.

Center rib roasts, sirloin roasts, loin roasts, tenderloins, and all types of **chops** and **ribs** should be roasted, grilled, or broiled over high heat. They all make good roast pork, with the loin roast being the leanest of the three. We also cut **pork chops** from the loin roasts. Whole **pork loins** often go on sale, and since they are boneless, you can easily cut them into boneless chops for less than half the price of ones the butcher cuts.

Tenderloins are small, generally 1 to 2 lb/455 to 910 g, and very tender. They can be roasted, grilled, or cut into medallions and sautéed. Either way, they cook quickly and are perfect for a weekday meal.

There are three types of ribs that are cut from the rib section of pigs: **country-style ribs, back ribs,** and **spareribs.** Country-style ribs are very meaty and have the great flavor of rib meat, but they can be eaten with a knife and fork. They are the least expensive type of ribs. They come boneless or bone-in and are great baked or grilled. Back ribs or baby back ribs are what you usually get if you order ribs in a restaurant. They have shorter rib bones, and the meat is mostly between the ribs. They are the most expensive of the three types of ribs. Spareribs have longer rib bones and usually have the rib cartilage at the top. Some restaurants cut the tops off and sell them as rib tips. Back ribs or spareribs are usually grilled.

Hams/gammons are sold whole or cut in half as shank or butt portions. The flavor is the same throughout, but the shank portion has a larger bone so it generally costs less than the butt portion.

WHITE BEAN SOUP

Megan I don't think there is really anything better in the winter than a nice bowl of hot soup. I know some people don't think soup is a filling meal, but, with the beans and Italian sausage, this soup is guaranteed to leave you satisfied. Not only that, but with all of the veggies, this soup makes sure you are getting in a good serving of greens!

2 leeks

3 stalks celery

2 carrots

3 cloves garlic

8 oz/225 g hot Italian sausage

One 15-oz/430-g can diced tomatoes, juices reserved

Three 14-oz/400-g cans vegetable broth

Two 15-oz/430-g cans white beans

½ cup/40 g frozen spinach

1 tbsp fresh lemon juice

½ tsp dried rosemary

Salt and pepper

Cut the roots and dark green from the leeks and slice in half lengthwise. Rinse under running water to remove any dirt and roughly chop the leeks. Cut the celery into slices ¼ in/6 mm thick. Peel the carrots and cut into slices ¼ in/6 mm thick. Peel and finely chop the garlic.

Squeeze the sausage out of the casings into a large sauce-pan. Cook over medium heat for 5 minutes, or until the meat begins to brown. Add the leeks, celery, and carrots and cook for 10 minutes, or until the leeks are translucent. Add the garlic and tomatoes with their juices, and cook for 3 minutes. Add the broth, stir well, and bring to a simmer. Drain and rinse the beans. Add the beans, spinach, lemon juice, and rosemary and season with salt and pepper. Bring to a boil, reduce the heat to low, and simmer 30 minutes, until the tomatoes have broken down. Ladle the soup into bowls and serve hot.

Lingo

Cooking the leeks as we did in this recipe is called "sweating." Sweat means to cook food at a fairly low temperature with a small amount of fat until it is soft, but not brown.

BAKED HAM AND ASPARAGUS OMELET

Megan

Figuring out this recipe has been a dream of mine for years. Back in Illinois, we had a local breakfast place where all the food was great, but their frittata-like omelets were amazing! Even after we moved, every time we went back to visit, a trip to Our Kitchen was a requirement. Their omelets were like no other—so fluffy, and filled with gooey cheese and vegetables. Finally, after years of experimenting, we found that starting it on the stove and then baking it in the oven is the secret to getting the right amount of fluff. Just be sure your pan is ovenproof before you try it out, or you'll have quite a mess to clean up afterward!

1 lb/455 g asparagus spears

8 oz/225 g thick-sliced ham/gammon

8 large eggs

½ cup/120 ml milk

Salt and pepper

1 tbsp canola oil

1½ cups/170 g shredded Jack cheese

Preheat the oven to 400°F/200°C/gas mark 6.

Break the ends off of the asparagus and cut the spears into pieces 1 in/2.5 cm long. Put the asparagus in a microwave-safe bowl and add enough water to just cover the bottom. Cover tightly with plastic wrap/cling film and cook on high for 5 minutes, or until just tender. Drain off the water.

Cut the ham/gammon into cubes ¼ to ½ in/6 to 12 mm wide.

Put the eggs and milk in a bowl and beat with a fork until completely combined. Season with salt and pepper. Add the asparagus and ham/gammon and stir well.

Heat the canola oil in a large, ovenproof frying pan over medium heat. Add the egg mixture and sprinkle the cheese over the eggs. Cook for 5 minutes. Put the pan in the oven and bake for 15 minutes more, or until the eggs are cooked through and fluffy. Cut omelet into four wedges and serve immediately.

141

On the Lighter Side

Even with all the cheese, this omelet comes in at just under 500 calories. If you drop the cheese down to 1 cup/115 g, which is still plenty, it goes down to 440 calories. And, if you want to skip the cheese completely, it goes down to 315 calories per serving. Personally, I think knocking down the amount of cheese is okay. Eliminating it, though—not a chance.

A.M. BLT SANDWICH

Jill   This is a super-delicious morning treat that's a twist on the standard BLT sandwich. I like it equally well with prosciutto or bacon/streaky bacon, so take your pick. I usually use crusty sourdough or French bread, but you can also use sandwich bread. If you use larger slices of bread, you may want to use two eggs for each sandwich so there is enough egg to cover it.

1 clove garlic

4 slices bread

2 tbsp butter, at room temperature

8 slices cooked bacon/streaky bacon or 4 slices prosciutto

1 cup/30 g loosely packed spring mix

1 tomato

4 eggs

Peel the garlic. Toast the bread slices in a toaster or under the broiler until golden brown. Rub the garlic over the toasted bread and then spread the slices with 1 tbsp of the butter. Place two slices of bacon or one slice of prosciutto on each piece of bread and top with some of the spring mix. Cut the tomato into eight thin slices and place two slices on each sandwich.

Melt the remaining 1 tbsp butter in a large frying pan over medium heat. Crack the eggs directly into the pan, keeping them separate. Cook for 3 minutes and then turn them over with a spatula, being careful not to break the yolks. Cook for 1 to 2 minutes more, or until the whites are cooked, but the yolks are still runny. Place an egg on top of each open-faced sandwich and serve immediately.

PULLED PORK SANDWICHES WITH COLESLAW

Jill

I always make a double batch of this pulled pork. The butt or shoulder roasts usually weigh about 6 lb/2.7 kg, so you can cook half now and half later or all now and have a quick meal later. It takes no extra time. Sounds like a no brainer to me! If you watch for the meat to go on sale, you can make these sandwiches for pocket change. It's delicious and inexpensive—the perfect combo.

COLESLAW

3 tbsp brown sugar

¾ cup/180 ml mayonnaise

3 tbsp milk

2 tbsp cider vinegar

½ tsp garlic powder

½ tsp ground mustard

8 oz/225 g shredded coleslaw mix

½ cup/85 g dried cranberries

SANDWICHES

3 lb/1.4 kg pork butt or shoulder

2 tbsp brown sugar

3 tbsp dry Cajun seasoning

1 cup/240 ml barbecue sauce

8 hamburger buns

To prepare the coleslaw: Put the brown sugar, mayonnaise, milk, vinegar, garlic powder, and ground mustard in a bowl and stir until combined. Add the coleslaw mix and cranberries and stir until completely coated. Refrigerate until ready to serve.

To prepare the sandwiches: Preheat the oven to 350°F/180°C/ gas mark 4.

Cut the pork into chunks 4 in/10 cm long and remove any excess fat. Combine the brown sugar and the Cajun seasoning in the bottom of a 9-by-13-inch/23-by-32-cm baking dish. Dredge the meat in the mixture on all sides and arrange the meat in the pan, leaving any excess rub behind. Add about ½ in/12 mm water to the pan and cover tightly with aluminum foil. Bake for 2½ hours, or until the meat is very tender.

Remove the meat from the pan and shred with a fork. Stir together the pork and barbecue sauce in a saucepan and cook over low heat for 10 minutes, or until hot.

Spoon the pulled pork onto the buns and serve immediately with the coleslaw.

ITALIAN SAUSAGE AND PEPPERS WITH WARM POTATO SALAD

Jill

Why is it that sausages come five to a pack and the buns always come with six or eight? And, why are the buns always two inches longer than the sausage? Whether it's a plot by the bun makers to get you to buy more than you need or just poor planning, I don't know. All I know is that it irritates me enough that I stopped buying buns. I buy baguettes and cut them to the length I want.

POTATO SALAD

1½ lb/680 g small red potatoes (about 10)

1 bunch green/spring onions (about 6)

3 tbsp Dijon mustard

3 tbsp olive oil

Salt and pepper

ITALIAN SAUSAGE AND PEPPERS

2 green bell peppers/capsicums

1 lb/455 g Italian sausage links

One 14-oz/400-g can beef broth

One 16- to 20-oz/455- to 570-g French baguette

To prepare the potato salad: Cut the potatoes in quarters and put them in a saucepan of salted water. Bring to a boil and cook over medium heat for 15 minutes, or until tender. Drain and keep warm.

Meanwhile, thinly slice the white and light green parts of the green/spring onions and put them in a bowl. Add the mustard and olive oil and stir until combined. Season with salt and pepper and stir in the warm potatoes.

To prepare the Italian sausage and peppers: Halve, seed, and cut the bell peppers/capsicums into slices ½ in/12 mm thick.

Put the sausage in a large frying pan and cook over high heat for 5 minutes, or until browned on both sides. Add the broth and bell peppers/capsicums, cover, and cook over medium-low heat for 20 minutes, or until the vegetables are very soft.

Cut the baguette into five pieces and slice them open, leaving a ¾ in/2 cm hinge on one side. Place a sausage on each roll and spoon the vegetables and juice over the bread.

Serve immediately with the potato salad.

DUBLIN CODDLE

Jill

I had this for the first time in Dublin, Ireland. I was initially skeptical but found out that this is a classic comfort food for the Irish—comparable, in my mind, to chicken and dumplings in the United States. More traditional versions don't have carrots or parsley, but we're not Irish, so we can get away with adding different stuff!

1 lb/455 g bacon/streaky bacon

1 lb/455 g white sausage, such as Thüringer or stadium bratwurst

2 onions

2 lb/910 g russet potatoes (4 or 5)

3 carrots

2 cloves garlic

4 cups/960 ml beef broth or apple cider

Salt and pepper

¼ cup/10 g chopped fresh parsley

Cut the bacon into pieces 1 in/2.5 cm long and put them in a large frying pan. Cook over medium-high heat, stirring occasionally, for 10 minutes, or until browned but not crisp. Drain the fat from the pan and put the bacon in a large saucepan.

Cut the sausage into chunks 2 in/5 cm long and put them in the frying pan. Cook over medium-high heat for 5 minutes, or until browned on all sides. Add the sausage to the saucepan.

Peel the onions and cut them into slices ¼ in/6 mm thick. Peel the potatoes and slice them about ¼ in/6 mm thick. Peel the carrots and cut them into pieces 2 in/5 cm long. Peel and roughly chop the garlic. Add the onions, potatoes, carrots, and garlic to the saucepan, pour in the broth, and season with salt and pepper. Cover and cook over medium heat for 1 hour. Remove the cover from the pan and cook for 30 minutes more, or until the liquid is reduced to about 3 cups/480 ml (see below). Stir in the parsley and serve immediately.

Lingo

Reduce means exactly what it sounds like—to make it less. When you cook liquids, evaporation occurs, making the flavors of the remaining liquid more intense. Instructions to reduce a liquid usually include how much liquid should be left. Those numbers are approximate, there is no need to measure, just eyeball it. If eyeballing it makes you nervous, before you start cooking measure the amount of liquid and put it in the pan to see how deep it is. Once you add the other ingredients, it will about double that. Remember: it's approximate, not exact.

HAM AND GOUDA CRÊPES
WITH GARLIC CREAM SAUCE

Jill

Who doesn't like crêpes? No one I know. I think it's probably because crêpes are so light and versatile. These crêpes are savory with a light garlic cream sauce, but it's the same crêpe you would make if you were filling them with fruit and whipped cream or topping with a sauce. Delicious.

CRÊPES

3 eggs

1 cup/240 ml milk

¾ cup/85 g flour

3 tbsp canola oil

¼ tsp salt

7 oz/200 g Gouda cheese

8 thin slices deli ham/gammon

SAUCE

2 cloves garlic

2 tbsp butter

2 tbsp flour

1½ cups/360 ml milk

Salt and pepper

To prepare the crêpes: Put the eggs, milk, flour, 2 tbsp of the canola oil, and the salt in a blender and pulse until completely smooth.

Pour the remaining 1 tbsp oil onto a paper towel/absorbent paper. Rub it over the bottom of an 8-in/20-cm nonstick frying pan over medium-high heat. Pour ¼ cup/60 ml of the batter into the pan and swirl it around to coat the entire bottom of the pan (see Cooking Tip, facing page). Cook for 2 minutes, or until the crêpe is set in the center. Turn over the crêpe and cook for 1 minute more, until lightly browned. Transfer the crêpe to a plate. Continue with the remaining batter.

Cut the cheese into slices ⅛ in/3 mm thick. Lay the ham/gammon on a flat surface and put several slices of cheese lengthwise down the center of each piece. Fold in the sides of the meat, completely covering the cheese. Put the frying pan over medium-low heat, lay the meat slices into the pan, folded-side down, and cook for 3 minutes, or until the cheese is melted.

To prepare the sauce: Peel and finely chop the garlic. Put the butter in a small saucepan and melt it over medium-high heat. Stir in the garlic and cook for 30 seconds. Add the 2 tbsp flour and cook, stirring constantly, for 1 minute, or until bubbly. Slowly stir in the milk and bring it to a boil. Cook for 1 minute and season with salt and pepper to finish the béchamel sauce (see Lingo, page 67).

Place one of the pieces of ham/gammon and cheese in the center of each crêpe and fold both sides over the ham. Place two crêpes on each plate and spoon the sauce over the crêpes.

Serve immediately.

Crêpes are thin and can rip easily. To keep from mangling them, make sure the pan is hot enough when you put in the batter. If you are impatient, you will end up mutilating the first crêpe you make. (Don't feel bad, though; my mom does this every single time she makes them.) Once the pan is hot, pour in the batter and swirl it around to cover the bottom. If you have any holes, dip a spoon in the batter and rub the back of the spoon over the hole to fill it in. Don't worry, these spots won't show once it's cooked. Wait until the center is set and the edges start to look dry and pull away from the pan. Then slide a rubber spatula under the edge and flip it over. (Sometimes it's easier to slide the tip of the spatula under the edge, then grab the edge with your fingers and hold the crêpe up a little so you can slide the spatula under the crêpe without having it fold up like an accordion.) It doesn't need to cook long on the second side—just enough to give it some color. It may take you a few tries to get the hang of it, but we allowed for that. You only need eight crêpes for this recipe, but the batter will make twelve.

JERK PORK CHOPS WITH CHIPOTLE MASHED POTATOES

Jill

This dish is packed with flavor, but we went light on the heat. If you like a little more zip, you can sprinkle the chops with a teaspoon of cayenne pepper before coating them with the marinade and increase the chipotles in the potatoes. Just be careful with the chipotles and add them a little at a time. They can make a dish quickly go from not zippy enough to mouth-burning hot.

PORK CHOPS

4 green/spring onions

2 jalapeño peppers

2 cloves garlic

2 tbsp fresh lemon or lime juice

1 tsp salt

1 tsp ground allspice

¼ tsp ground cinnamon

4 thick-cut pork chops

MASHED POTATOES

2 lb/910 g russet potatoes (4 to 5)

2 cloves garlic

¼ cup/55 g butter

½ cup/120 ml milk

1 chipotle pepper in adobo sauce

Salt and pepper

To prepare the pork chops: Thinly slice the white and light green parts of the green/spring onions. Halve, seed, and finely chop the jalapeños. Peel and finely chop the garlic. Put the onions, jalapeños, garlic, lemon juice, salt, allspice, and cinnamon in a medium bowl and stir until combined. Spread the mixture over both sides of the pork chops and put them in a baking dish or a resealable plastic bag. Refrigerate for at least 2 hours or up to 8 hours.

To prepare the mashed potatoes: Peel the potatoes and cut them into chunks. Put the potatoes in a large saucepan of salted water, add the garlic, and cook over medium heat for 20 minutes, or until the potatoes are tender. Drain off the water and return the pan to the stove. Add the butter and milk to the pan and cook over medium heat until the milk comes to a boil. Smash the potatoes and garlic with a fork or potato masher until fairly smooth. Finely dice the chipotle and stir it into the potatoes. Season with salt and pepper. Keep warm.

Preheat a grill/barbecue or grill pan on high heat.

Put the pork chops on the grill/barbecue and cook for 4 to 5 minutes on each side, or until the centers are no longer pink.

Place a pork chop and some of the mashed potatoes on each plate and serve immediately.

> ## Cooking Tip

When you're using a marinade that contains an acid such as lemon juice, lime juice, or vinegar, it's important to use a nonreactive pan. Metals such as copper and aluminum will react with the acid, causing your food to have a metallic taste. Of course, those are the metals that conduct heat well, so they are often used in making pots and pans. Glass, plastic, or stainless steel are all nonreactive and will keep your food tasting great.

BREADED PORK CHOPS WITH RICE PILAF

Jill

When I was little and my dad made dinner, this is usually what he made. The pork chops are nice and crunchy on the outside and juicy on the inside. I usually have them with applesauce on the side so it's a little bit sweet, too. Combined with the rice pilaf, one of my favorite foods on the planet, this dish is perfect comfort food.

RICE PILAF

1 small onion

1 carrot

1 stalk celery

2 tbsp butter

½ cup/100 g dry orzo

3 cups/720 ml chicken broth

1 cup/215 g dry rice

1 tsp salt

PORK CHOPS

Cooking spray

⅓ cup/40 g flour

Salt and pepper

1 large egg

¾ cup/65 g cornflake crumbs

4 pork chops

To prepare the rice pilaf: Peel the onion and carrot and cut them into slices ¼ in/6 mm thick. Remove the ends from the celery and cut it into slices ¼ in/6 mm thick.

Melt the butter in a large saucepan over medium-high heat. Add the orzo and cook, stirring frequently, for 5 minutes, or until golden brown. Add the onion, carrot, celery, broth, rice, and salt and bring to a boil. Reduce to medium-low heat, cover, and cook for 20 minutes, or until the rice is tender.

To prepare the pork chops: Preheat the oven to 350°F/180°C/gas mark 4. Lightly coat a baking sheet/tray with cooking spray or oil.

Put the flour in a shallow bowl and season with salt and pepper. Put the egg and 2 tbsp water in a shallow bowl and beat until completely combined. Put the cornflake crumbs in a third shallow bowl. Dredge (see Lingo, page 78) both sides of the pork chops in the flour, then the egg, and then the cornflake crumbs. Put the pork chops in the prepared baking dish and bake for 15 minutes. Turn over the chops and cook for 10 minutes more, or until no longer pink in the center.

Place a pork chop on each plate and serve with the pilaf on the side.

Ingredient Info

Orzo is a small football-shaped pasta that is often used in soups. We like to use it for rice pilaf because it is similar in size to the rice and it browns well, giving the dish more color.

SWEET AND SOUR PORK

Megan

Normally, sweet and sour is something I would only order at a restaurant. It's a pain to deep-fry the meat, and without the breading it just isn't the same. Then I came up with this version. The breading is actually the marinade and it is as simple as mixing a couple of ingredients together in a bowl. The long ingredient list makes this recipe look hard, but most of the items are just stirred together for the marinade and the sauce. Trust me; it's really not hard to make.

MARINADE

2 cloves garlic

1 lb/455 g boneless country-style ribs

½ cup/60 g flour

⅓ cup/75 ml soy sauce

¼ cup/30 g cornstarch/cornflour

2 tbsp finely chopped peeled fresh ginger

Salt and pepper

Canola oil, for frying

RICE

1 cup/215 g dry white rice

2¼ cups/540 ml water

SAUCE

1 large onion

1 red bell pepper/capsicum

1 green bell pepper/capsicum

1 carrot

One 20-oz/570-g can pineapple chunks, juice reserved

One 6-oz/180-ml can pineapple juice

2 tbsp rice wine vinegar

2 tbsp soy sauce

2 tbsp cornstarch/cornflour

1 tbsp tomato sauce

1 tbsp honey

1 tbsp canola oil

To prepare the marinade: Peel and finely chop the garlic. Cut the ribs into cubes 1 in/2.5 cm long.

Combine the garlic, ¼ cup/30 g of the flour, the soy sauce, cornstarch/cornflour, ginger, and 2 tbsp water. Add the ribs, toss until completely coated, and marinate for 30 minutes.

Put the remaining ¼ cup/30 g flour in a shallow bowl and season with salt and pepper. Drain the marinade from the ribs and dredge the pork in the flour. Pour ¾ in/2 cm of oil into a large frying pan and cook over high heat until very hot (about 375°F/190°C on a deep-fat thermometer); a small drop of water added to the pan should immediately begin to bubble. Put some of the ribs in the pan, but do not crowd the meat or it will cook too slowly and become greasy. Cook for 3 to 4 minutes, or until golden brown. Drain the pork on paper towels/absorbent paper. Continue with the remaining meat.

To prepare the rice: Put the rice and water in a small saucepan and bring to a boil. Cover and cook over low heat for 20 minutes, or until the rice is tender. Keep warm.

To prepare the sauce: Peel the onion and chop it into pieces 1 in/2.5 cm long. Halve, seed, and cut the bell peppers/capsicums into pieces 1 in/2.5 cm long. Peel the carrot, cut it in half lengthwise, and thinly slice it on a diagonal.

Combine the two pineapple juices, vinegar, soy sauce, cornstarch/cornflour, tomato sauce, and honey in a small bowl.

Put the canola oil in a large frying pan over medium-high heat. Add the onion, bell peppers/capsicums, and carrot and cook for 5 minutes, or until slightly softened. Add the sauce and cook for 15 minutes, or until the sauce is thick. Stir in the meat and pineapple chunks and remove the pan from the heat.

Spoon some of the rice onto each plate and top with the pork.

SWEET AND SPICY PORK TENDERLOIN WITH MASHED SWEET POTATOES

Megan

Pork tenderloins are the perfect choice for a quick weekday meal. They are fast and easy to prepare, and the meat is extremely tender and juicy. Watch carefully when you buy them though; the last time I purchased one the first thing I saw was an expensive pre-seasoned name-brand version. While I was reeling from shock, I noticed the store brand right below it for less than half the price. I think you can figure out which one I bought.

PORK TENDERLOIN

1 chipotle pepper in adobo sauce

½ cup/150 g peach or apricot preserves

1 pork tenderloin (about 1½ lb/680 g)

Salt and pepper

1 tbsp olive oil

SWEET POTATOES

3 sweet potatoes

1 tbsp butter

½ tsp ground cinnamon

To prepare the pork tenderloin: Preheat the oven to 400°F/200°C/gas mark 6.

Finely chop the chipotle and put in a small bowl with the preserves. Stir until combined.

Season the tenderloin with salt and pepper. Heat the olive oil in a frying pan over high heat. Add the tenderloin and cook for 1 minute on all sides, or until browned. Put the tenderloin on a baking sheet/tray and spread the top and sides with one half of the preserves mixture, reserving the remainder for later. Bake for 25 minutes, or until the internal temperature reaches 140°F/60°C for medium-rare or 150°F/65°C for well-done. Remove from the oven and let the tenderloin rest for 10 minutes (the internal temperature will rise to approximately 155°F/68°C while it rests).

To prepare the sweet potatoes: Peel the sweet potatoes and cut them into chunks. Put the potatoes in a saucepan of salted water and cook over medium-high heat for 20 minutes, or until soft. Drain off the water and return the sweet potatoes to the pan. Add the butter and cinnamon and mash everything together with a fork or potato masher until smooth.

Heat the reserved preserves mixture in a microwave-safe bowl for 1 minute, or until warm.

Spoon some of the potatoes on each plate. Cut the tenderloins into slices ¼ in/6 mm thick. Shingle the slices on the potatoes and spoon some of the warmed preserves down the center. Serve immediately.

variation BLACKENED PORK TENDERLOIN

Rub 2 tbsp dry Cajun seasoning on the pork loin before searing and don't use the preserves mixture.

CARNITAS

Jill

Carnitas, or shredded pork, is usually something I get when I go out, so, when I decided to make it at home, I was surprised at how easy it was. It took a few minutes to cut up the meat but, once that was done, it basically sat in the oven for a few hours. When it was done, it was so tender it literally fell apart. Just be careful with how much salt you put on it. I definitely put on too much the first time I made it. Oops.

3 lb/1.4 kg pork butt or shoulder

Salt

4 cloves garlic

1 jalapeño pepper

1 bunch cilantro/fresh coriander

One 12-oz/360-ml can beer

2 tomatoes

1 small onion

Twelve 6-in/15-cm flour tortillas

1 cup/115 g shredded Cheddar or Jack cheese

Preheat the oven to 350°F/180°C/gas mark 4.

Cut the pork into chunks 4 in/10 cm long and remove any excess fat. Season the chunks lightly with salt and put them in a 9-by-13-in/23-by-32-cm baking dish. Peel the garlic and cut in half, and add to the dish. Slice the jalapeño in half, leaving the seeds in and add it to the dish. Finely chop ¼ cup/10 g of the cilantro/fresh coriander and set it aside for later use. Roughly chop the remaining herb and sprinkle it over the meat. Pour the beer into the dish and cover tightly with aluminum foil. Bake for 3 hours, or until the meat is very tender. Remove the meat from the dish and shred into bite-size pieces with a fork.

Halve, seed, and cut the tomatoes into pieces ½ in/12 mm long. Peel the onion and cut it into slices ¼ in/6 mm wide.

Place some of the meat on each tortilla and top it with the tomatoes, onion, cheese, and the reserved cilantro/fresh coriander. Eat immediately.

> **Cooking Tip**

Cross-contamination is carrying bacteria from one object to another, and it is the most common cause of foodborne illness at home. It can happen if you use the same utensils on uncooked and cooked food. However, it is easy to avoid by taking a few simple steps. Wash your hands frequently when cooking, particularly after working with raw meat. Wash your cutting board and knife with very hot soapy water after cutting raw meat or poultry. Don't use the same plates or containers for raw and cooked food without washing them well in between. And, don't forget the sponge or dish/tea towels. If you use one to wipe up after cutting meat, throw it in the laundry basket and grab a clean one.

Chapter 7

DESSERTS

Baking is a science . . . literally. With things like ratios, acidity, and viscosity to be considered, you may feel more like a chemist than a cook. Fortunately for us, someone else figured out all of that stuff a long time ago. We just have to follow the recipes. In the other chapters, we have encouraged you to experiment and change recipes to suit your tastes. That stops here. Baking is a series of chemical reactions and changing amounts or types of ingredients changes those reactions. Sometimes it works out okay, but more often it doesn't.

We don't mean to scare you away from baking; we just want you to use a little caution. Your best bet for good results is to make the recipes as they are written. But, if you're one of those people who have to try it their way (that would be us), start slow. Make a recipe a few times before you consider making any changes and then think about the structure of the dessert. The Yellow Butter Cake (page 163) has a thicker batter that makes a fairly dense cake. We added apples to it without any problem. On the other hand, if we added apples to the Angel Food Cake (page 170), it would fall flatter than a pancake. It's that science thing again.

There are a few things we've learned during our forays into baking that will hopefully keep you from making the same mistakes we've made:

- Measure everything exactly.

- Use dry measuring cups for dry ingredients and liquid measuring cups for liquids. Yes, there is a difference. A liquid measure is slightly more than a dry measure and usually comes with a spout and handle.

- Stir flour before measuring to loosen it up. If it has any lumps, sift it or pass it through a strainer to break them up.

- Flour and sugar should be scooped into the cup and leveled off with a knife.

- Brown sugar should be firmly packed into the cup.

- Chocolate can develop a white film on the outside called "bloom" that is caused by temperature variations. It does not affect the flavor or texture of the chocolate, and it's still fine to use.

- Prepare the pan before mixing the cake. Once the batter is mixed, the leavening bubbles start to form. Pouring the batter after it has been sitting for a few minutes will break the bubbles and result in a denser cake.

- Eggs added to hot liquids must be tempered (warmed a little) or they become scrambled.

- Eggs separate best when they are cold, but egg whites whip up better when they are at room temperature. So separate them straight from the refrigerator and let them sit for a bit before whipping.

- Toss nuts or dried fruit in flour before adding them to batter to keep them from falling to the bottom of the cake.

- Preheat the oven. Baking desserts before the oven is up to temperature can cause them to form a hard outer layer that is unpleasant to eat, and it will keep desserts from rising properly.

- Reduce the oven temperature by 25°F/15°C for glass pans. Glass heats more quickly and retains heat longer than metal.

- Don't overmix the ingredients once the flour has been added. The gluten in the flour can become too elastic and keep cakes from rising.

- Bake desserts in the center of the oven. The back, top, and bottom of the oven can be hotter than the center. If you know your oven heats unevenly, rotate the pan halfway through cooking. If your cakes bake unevenly, buy an inexpensive oven thermometer and place it different spots in your oven to find the most true heat.

- Make sure a cake is finished baking before removing it from the oven. If you take it out too early and it starts to fall, you'll be eating underdone cake. Putting it back in the oven won't help. The chemical reaction that causes bubbles to form has stopped and will not start again. It should spring back when gently pressed in the center.

- If the center of your cake forms a peak and cracks, your oven temperature is too high.

- To remove a cake from the pan, run a knife around the edge of the pan, place a wire rack on top of the cake, hold the rack and pan together, flip them over, and then remove the pan.

- It's easy to get sidetracked and forget to take your cake out of the pan while it's still hot. If this happens, simply put the cake pan/tin on the stove over low heat for a minute or so, moving it around constantly, to melt the butter or oil in the bottom of the pan. The cake will then release from the pan with no problems.

- If you have a lot of crumbs when frosting a cake, spread a thin layer of frosting over the cake to hold down the crumbs and then go back and add another layer of frosting.

YELLOW BUTTER CAKE

Jill

This is a delicious cake that is easy to make and, more important, hard to ruin. It is dense enough for even a novice at layer cakes to easily handle without breaking it apart. Those of you that feel the need to experiment with adding nuts, chips, or fruit, this is the place to start. The apple-pecan variation is pictured on page 165.

Cooking spray

1 cup/225 g butter, at room temperature

2 cups/400 g sugar

4 large eggs

1 tbsp vanilla extract

4 tsp baking powder

1 tsp salt

3 cups/385 g all-purpose/plain flour

1½ cups/360 ml milk

Preheat the oven to 350°F/180°C/gas mark 4. Coat a 9-by-13-in/ 23-by-32-cm baking pan or two 8-in/20-cm cake pans/tins with cooking spray or line 24 cupcake/fairy cake cups with paper liners.

Put the butter and sugar in a large bowl and beat them with an electric mixer on medium speed for 1 minute, or until completely smooth. Add the eggs one at a time, beating well after each addition. Add the vanilla, baking powder, and salt and mix on low speed until combined. Alternate adding half of the flour and half of the milk to the bowl and mix on low speed after each addition until combined. When all of the milk and flour have been incorporated, turn the mixer to high speed and mix for 1 minute, or until completely smooth.

Pour the batter into the prepared pans/tins and bake until the cake springs back when gently pressed in the center, 15 to 20 minutes for cupcakes/fairy cakes, 25 to 30 minutes for 8-in/20-cm layers, and 30 to 40 minutes for a 9-by-13-in/ 23-by-32-cm baking pan. For layer cakes, cool them in the pans/tins for 10 minutes and then remove the cakes to cooling racks. Cool completely before frosting.

variation CINNAMON CRUMBLE CAKE

Mix ¼ cup/55 g butter, ¾ cup/85 g flour, ¾ cup/150 g firmly packed brown sugar, and 2 tbsp ground cinnamon with a fork until crumbly. Pour half of the batter into a prepared 9-by-13-in/ 23-by-32-cm baking pan and sprinkle it with half of the cinnamon crumble. Pour the remaining batter into the pan and top with the remaining crumble. Bake as directed.

(continued)

variation ORANGE CAKE

Instead of all milk, use ½ cup/120 ml fresh orange juice and 1 cup/240 ml milk and add 2 tsp finely grated orange zest with the flour. Frost with Orange Buttercream Frosting (page 175). This also makes a great lemon cake by substituting lemon juice and zest for the orange.

variation APPLE-PECAN CAKE

Make the batter as directed. Peel and thinly slice 4 apples (see below) and stir them into the batter. Combine ¾ cup/150 g firmly packed brown sugar with ¾ cup/85 g chopped pecans and sprinkle over the cake. Bake as directed. Combine 1 cup/100 g confectioners'/icing sugar with 1½ tbsp milk and drizzle over the cooled cake.

Ingredient Info

There are so many types of apples out there that it's hard to keep them straight. I used to stand in the produce section trying to remember which kind was supposed to be best for what. If you look up types of apples, you'll find that the experts say Red Delicious, Gala, and Fuji are considered the best eating apples and Granny Smith, Golden Delicious, and Jonathan are best for cooking. But the reality is that any of these will work fine for baking except Red Delicious. They are too soft and get mushy when baked.

FAVORITE CHOCOLATE CAKE

Megan If you make this recipe as it is written, this cake is light and fluffy and makes the best chocolate cupcakes/fairy cakes I've ever had. However, it can also be made as a "dump" cake, which means that all of the ingredients are dumped into a bowl and mixed at one time. The cake will be a little more dense, but it still will be delicious.

Cooking spray

¾ cup/170 g butter, at room temperature

²/₃ cup/130 g granulated sugar

²/₃ cup/130 g firmly packed brown sugar

3 large eggs

2 tsp vanilla extract

½ cup/50 g unsweetened cocoa

1 tsp baking soda/bicarbonate of soda

1 tsp baking powder

½ tsp salt

2 cups/255 g all-purpose/plain flour

1½ cups/360 ml milk

Preheat the oven to 350°F/180°C/gas mark 4. Coat a 9-by-13-in/23-by-32-cm baking pan or two 8-in/20-cm cake pans/tins with cooking spray or line 24 cupcake/fairy cake cups with paper liners.

Put the butter, granulated sugar, and brown sugar in a large bowl and beat them with an electric mixer on low speed for 1 minute, or until the sugar is incorporated. Add the eggs and mix on high speed for 2 minutes, or until fluffy. Add the vanilla and mix well. Add the cocoa, baking soda/bicarbonate of soda, baking powder, and salt and mix on low speed for 30 seconds, or until incorporated. Alternate adding half of the flour and half of the milk to the bowl and mix on low speed after each addition until combined. When all of the milk and flour have been incorporated, turn the mixer to high speed and mix for 1 minute, or until completely smooth.

Pour the batter into the prepared pans/tins and bake until the cake springs back when gently pressed in the center, 18 to 23 minutes for cupcakes/fairy cakes, 30 to 35 minutes for 8-in/20-cm layers, and 35 to 45 minutes for a 9-by-13-in/23-by-32-cm baking pan. For layer cakes, cool them in the pans/tins for 10 minutes and then remove the cakes to cooling racks. Cool completely before frosting.

variation MOCHA CAKE

Substitute double-strength coffee or espresso for the milk and bake as directed. This cake will be a little more dense and more moist than the regular chocolate cake.

variation NO-FROST CAKE

Pour the batter into a greased 9-by-13-in/23-by-32-cm baking pan and sprinkle it with 1 cup/170 g chocolate chips and 1 cup/115 g chopped pecans or walnuts to eliminate the need for frosting.

FLUFFY WHITE CAKE

Jill

This cake is lighter than the Yellow Butter Cake (page 163) or Favorite Chocolate Cake (facing page). That is partly because of the egg whites and partly because of the cake/soft-wheat flour, which is a lower protein version of all-purpose/plain flour. If you don't have any on hand, you can put 2 tbsp of cornstarch/cornflour in the bottom of a 1-cup/115-g measure and then fill the rest with well-sifted flour. Personally, I think it's easier to just buy the cake/soft-wheat flour. Like the Yellow and Chocolate Cakes, this is a master recipe that you can customize simply with berries or with fancier additions, such as the coconut variation shown on page 169.

Cooking spray

¾ cup/170 g butter, at room temperature

1½ cups/300 g sugar

1 tsp vanilla extract

2 tsp baking powder

2⅔ cups/305 g cake/soft-wheat flour

¾ cup/180 ml milk

6 large egg whites

Preheat the oven to 350°F/180°C/gas mark 4. Coat a 9-by-13-in/23-by-32-cm baking pan or two 8-in/20-cm cake pans/tins with cooking spray or line 24 cupcake/fairy cake cups with paper liners.

Put the butter and sugar in a large bowl and beat them with an electric mixer on low speed for 1 minute, or until the sugar is incorporated. Turn the mixer to high speed and beat for 2 minutes, or until fluffy. Add the vanilla and mix well. Add the baking powder and mix on low speed for 30 seconds, or until incorporated. Alternate adding half of the flour and half of the milk to the bowl and mix on low speed after each addition until combined. When all of the milk and flour have been incorporated, turn the mixer to high speed and mix for 1 minute, or until completely smooth.

Put the egg whites in a bowl and mix on high speed with clean beaters for 3 minutes, or until stiff peaks form. (When you lift the beaters out of the eggs, they should form peaks that stay upright.) Stir about one-quarter of the egg whites into the batter to loosen it up. Add the remaining egg whites to the batter and, using a spatula, fold the egg whites into the batter mixture by carefully sliding the spatula down one side of the pan, across the bottom, and pulling the batter up over the egg whites. Repeat the process until only a few streaks of egg white remain. Do not over-mix or the eggs will deflate.

Pour the batter into the prepared pans/tins and bake until the cake springs back when gently pressed in the center, 15 to 20 minutes for cupcakes/fairy cakes, 25 to 30 minutes for 8-in/20-cm layers, and 30 to 40 minutes for a 9-by-13-in/23-by-32-cm baking pan. For layer cakes, cool them in the pans/tins for 10 minutes and then remove the cakes to cooling racks. Cool completely before frosting.

(continued)

variation COCONUT CAKE

Bake the cake as directed. While the cake is baking, put one 13-oz/400-ml can of coconut milk and 3 tbsp sugar into a small saucepan and cook over medium heat for 5 minutes, or until the sugar is dissolved. Remove from the heat and let cool. Put 1 cup/ 120 g shredded/dessicated sweetened coconut on a cake pan/tin and bake, stirring occasionally, for 8 minutes, or until toasted. Put a piece of waxed/greaseproof paper under the cooling racks and turn the hot cakes out onto the racks. Poke holes in the cake with a skewer or large meat fork and spoon the coconut milk over the cake. Cool completely, frost with Buttercream Frosting (page 175), and sprinkle with the toasted coconut.

> ### Cooking Tip
>
> There are 3 tsp in 1 tbsp and 16 tbsp in 1 cup. That may not seem important, but, trust me, it will come in handy. For example, if you are substituting all-purpose/plain flour for the cake/soft-wheat flour in this recipe, removing 2 tbsp of flour from each cup is easy. But what do you do about the ⅔ cup? Well, since you now know that 3 tsp equals 1 tbsp, then 2 tbsp would be 6 tsp and two-thirds of 6 tsp is 4 tsp. That ends the math lesson for today.

168

ANGEL FOOD CAKE

Jill

Angel food cake is one of my all-time favorite summer desserts. It is so light and fluffy, which means that you can eat way more of it, right? My boyfriend has a theory that stomachs are divided into dinner and dessert sides, so you should always have room for dessert. With desserts like this, though, you don't have to worry about separate sides. There's always room for angel food cake. Make sure your bowl and utensils are impeccably clean for this one. Even the slightest bit of grease will keep the egg whites from whipping up properly.

1½ cups/360 ml large egg whites (about 12), at room temperature

1½ tsp cream of tartar

1½ tsp vanilla extract

¼ tsp salt

1½ cups/300 g sugar

1 cup/115 g cake/soft-wheat flour

Preheat the oven to 375°F/190°C/gas mark 5.

Put the egg whites in a large bowl and beat with an electric mixer on high speed for 1 minute, or until frothy. Add the cream of tartar, vanilla, and salt and mix on high speed for 2 minutes, or until soft peaks form. Sprinkle in the sugar and mix on high speed for 1 minute, or until stiff peaks form. Sprinkle the flour over the egg whites and gently fold it in.

Pour the batter into an ungreased tube pan and bake for 45 minutes, or until the top is golden brown and looks dry. Remove from the oven and invert the pan with the cake in it onto a bottle until completely cool. Removing the cake from the pan before it is cool can cause it to fall. Run a sharp knife around the edge and remove the bottom and tube insert from the pan if they are removable. Run the knife around the base of the insert and invert the cake onto a serving plate.

Make the angel food cake as directed and cool it completely. Beat 1 cup/240 ml heavy/double cream until soft peaks form. Add ¼ cup/20 g confectioners'/icing sugar and beat until stiff peaks form. Smash 1 cup/115 g thawed frozen strawberries with a fork, leaving them fairly chunky, and stir them into the whipped cream. Using a serrated knife, cut the top 2 in/5 cm off of the cake and set it aside. Make a cut about 2 in/5 cm deep and ¾ in/2 cm away from the outer edge of the cake. Repeat the cut, staying ¾ in/2 cm from the center of the cake. Make a cross cut to connect the lines and insert a fork into the cut. Gently pull out the center of the cake between the two cuts, forming a trench inside the cake. Fill the trench with the whipped cream mixture, reserving about ½ cup/120 ml for the top. Place the top back on the cake and spread the remaining whipped cream mixture evenly over the top of the cake. Refrigerate until ready to serve.

> ## Cooking Tip

Every time I make an angel food cake, I have the same problem . . . what to do with all the egg yolks. I was lamenting this to my grandmother the other day, and she asked why I didn't just put the yolks in the freezer. She puts them in small bags and marks how many are in there so she can use them later. I never knew you could do that, but now I do (and so do you).

LIQUID-CENTER CHOCOLATE CAKES

Megan

This cake is very rich and intensely chocolate, but it's not very sweet. I think it needs the ice cream to add a little sweetness and to cut the chocolate a little. These are best served hot out of the oven. If you want to serve them for guests, mix them up before you eat and pop them in the oven after dinner. If that's not possible, cook them for only 9 minutes and reheat them in the microwave for 30 seconds.

½ cup/115 g butter

5 oz/140 g bittersweet chocolate

4 large eggs

3 tbsp sugar

3 tbsp flour

Vanilla ice cream, for serving

Preheat the oven to 350°F/180°C/gas mark 4. Butter and flour four 3-in/8-cm ramekins.

Put the butter and chocolate in a microwave-safe bowl, cook on high heat for 2 minutes, and stir until smooth.

Put the eggs and sugar in a bowl and beat with an electric mixer on high speed for 3 minutes, or until light yellow and slightly thickened. Add the chocolate mixture to the eggs and mix on medium speed for 1 minute. Stir in the flour until incorporated and divide the batter among the prepared ramekins.

Bake for 10 minutes. Run a knife around the edges of the ramekins and invert them onto small plates. Place a scoop of ice cream on top of each cake and serve immediately.

PUMPKIN LOG

Jill

This cake is guaranteed to impress your friends with your culinary expertise, and it's really not hard to make. Just make sure to use a dish/tea towel to roll the cake; plastic wrap/cling film or parchment/baking paper seal in the steam that can make the cake soggy. And, if the cake cracks when you unroll it (yes, it happens to the best of us), don't put any of the filling in the cracks. That way when you roll it back up, the cracks will close up, and no one will even know they are there.

CAKE

Cooking spray

¼ cup/25 g confectioners'/icing sugar

3 large eggs

1 cup/200 g granulated sugar

⅔ cup/165 ml canned pumpkin

½ tsp baking powder

½ tsp ground cinnamon

½ tsp ground cloves

¼ tsp salt

¾ cup/85 g all-purpose/plain flour

FILLING

8 oz/225 g cream cheese, at room temperature

¼ cup/55 g butter, at room temperature

1 cup/100 g confectioners'/icing sugar

1 tsp vanilla extract

confectioners'/icing sugar, for sprinkling

Preheat the oven to 375°F/190°C/gas mark 5. Line a 10-by-15-in/ 25-by-38-cm baking sheet/tray with parchment/baking paper and lightly coat it with cooking spray or oil. Sprinkle a cotton dish/tea towel evenly with the confectioners'/icing sugar.

To make the cake: Put the eggs and granulated sugar in a large bowl and beat with an electric mixer on high speed for 2 minutes, or until thick. Add the pumpkin and mix on low speed for 1 minute, or until combined. Add the baking powder, cinnamon, cloves, and salt and mix for 1 minute, or until the spices are evenly distributed. Add the flour and mix on low speed for 1 minute, or until completely incorporated.

Using a rubber spatula, spread the batter evenly in the prepared pan and bake for 12 to 15 minutes, or until the cake springs back when gently pressed in the center. Remove the cake from the oven and invert it onto the prepared towel. Remove the paper and, starting at one of the short ends, carefully roll up the cake. Put the roll on a cooling rack with the end of the towel on the bottom and let it cool completely.

To make the filling: Put the cream cheese and butter in a bowl and mix with an electric mixer on medium speed for 2 minutes, or until completely smooth. Add the confectioners'/icing sugar and vanilla and mix for 1 minute, or until combined.

Carefully unroll the cake and spread the filling evenly over the entire cake. Reroll the cake and place it on a serving plate, seam-side down. Trim off the ends of the cake and sprinkle the top of the cake with confectioners'/icing sugar.

Cooking Tip

Cream cheese should always be completely smooth before adding any liquids. If there are any lumps in it when you add the liquid, they will be almost impossible to get out.

BUTTERCREAM FROSTING

Megan

Please, please, please—if you are taking the time to make a homemade cake, make homemade frosting. It is super-simple and so much better than the stuff in a can. This makes enough to frost a two-layer cake. Cut the recipe in half to frost a 9-by-13-in/ 23-by-32-cm cake or 24 cupcakes/fairy cakes.

¾ cup/170 g butter, at room temperature

1½ tsp vanilla extract

⅓ cup/75 ml milk

6 to 7 cups/600 to 700 g confectioners'/icing sugar

Put the butter in a large bowl and beat it with an electric mixer on medium speed for 1 minute, or until creamy. Add the vanilla and milk and mix on low speed until combined. Add 6 cups/ 600 g of the sugar and mix on low speed until the sugar is incorporated. Mix on medium speed for 1 minute, or until fluffy. Add the remaining 1 cup/100 g sugar a little at a time, mixing after each addition, until you reach a fluffy, spreadable consistency. (You may not need all of the sugar.) Any extra frosting can be refrigerated in an airtight container for up to 1 week. Mix with an electric mixer for 1 minute to make it fluffy again.

variation CHOCOLATE BUTTERCREAM FROSTING

Add ½ cup/50 g cocoa with the confectioners'/icing sugar.

variation ORANGE BUTTERCREAM FROSTING

Substitute ½ cup/120 ml fresh orange juice for the first addition of milk.

CREAMY RICE PUDDING

Megan

In my family, rice pudding always meant leftover rice baked with milk and eggs to form a solid, custard type dessert. The first time I saw this looser version of rice pudding was when I went to Germany. They call it "milk rice" and make it using Arborio rice, which gives it a creamy texture. I love to add cinnamon and sugar, but you can add fresh fruit, jelly, or even chocolate, and it is delicious.

4 cups/960 ml milk

1 cup/215 g dry short-grain rice, such as Arborio

½ tsp salt

½ cup/100 g sugar

3 large egg yolks

½ tsp ground cinnamon

½ cup/85 g raisins

1 tbsp vanilla extract

Put the milk, rice, and salt in a saucepan and bring to a boil. Reduce to medium-low heat, cover, and cook for 20 minutes, or until the rice is tender.

Put the sugar and egg yolks in a small bowl and stir well. Add a little of the milk mixture to the bowl and stir until combined to temper it (see below). Add the egg mixture to the pan and stir until evenly colored. Add the cinnamon and raisins and cook until the mixture just begins to bubble. Remove from the heat and stir in the vanilla. Cool slightly and serve warm.

The process of adding a small amount of hot liquid to the eggs before adding them to the pan is called "tempering." It allows the eggs to warm up before being added to the hot liquid. It is extremely important when dealing with eggs because, if you pour them straight into the hot liquid they will instantly begin to cook, and you'll have scrambled eggs.

CARAMEL-BANANA CREAM PIE

Jill

In my book, all banana cream pies are good, but with the layer of caramel, this one is definitely at the top of the heap. Even though this has a fair amount of ingredients, it's really not hard to make, and it's well worth the effort. I have given you the directions to make the pie crust, but prepared pie crusts are fine. I've used them three or four (dozen) times.

CRUST

1 cup/115 g all-purpose/plain flour

½ tsp salt

⅓ cup/75 g cold butter or shortening/vegetable lard

FILLING

2½ cups/600 ml milk

¾ cup/150 g sugar

¼ cup/30 g cornstarch/cornflour

¼ tsp salt

3 large egg yolks

2 tbsp butter

2 tsp vanilla extract

3 bananas

1 cup store-bought caramel sauce

TOPPING

1 cup/240 ml heavy/double cream

¼ cup/20 g confectioners'/icing sugar

To prepare the crust: Preheat the oven to 350°F/180°C/gas mark 4.

Put the flour and salt in a bowl. Cut the butter into cubes ½ in/12 mm long and add them to the bowl. Cut in the butter using two knives or a pastry cutter until it is the size of small peas (see Lingo, page 179). Add 3 tbsp very cold water and stir with a fork until the dough just begins to hold together. Press the dough into a disc ½ in/12 mm thick and put it on a floured work surface. Cover with plastic wrap/cling film and refrigerate for 15 minutes. Roll the dough into a circle about 11 in/28 cm wide. Fold the dough loosely in half and transfer it to a 9-in/23-cm pie pan. Unfold the dough and gently press it into the pan. Trim the edges of the dough, leaving a ¾ in/2 cm overhang at the edge of the pan. Fold the excess under itself and press with a fork all the way around to crimp the edge. Lay a piece of parchment/baking paper over the crust and add weights (see Lingo, page 179). Bake for 20 minutes, or until golden brown on the edges. Remove the paper and weights and allow the crust to cool on a rack.

To prepare the filling: Put the milk, sugar, cornstarch/cornflour, and salt in a saucepan over medium heat and bring to a boil. Boil for 1 minute. Beat the egg yolks in a small bowl. Remove the pan from the heat and stir a small amount of the hot liquid into the egg to temper it (see Lingo, facing page). Stir the egg mixture into the pan and cook over medium heat for 1 minute, or until it just begins to bubble. Remove the pan from the heat, add the butter and vanilla, and stir until combined. Let the pudding cool slightly.

(continued)

Cut the bananas into slices ¼ in/6 mm thick. Arrange some of the banana slices in a single layer on the pie crust. Spread the caramel over the bananas and spoon on half of the pudding. Top with the remaining bananas and spoon on the remaining pudding. Refrigerate until thoroughly chilled.

To prepare the topping: Put the cream in a bowl and beat with an electric mixer on high speed for 2 minutes, or until stiff peaks form. Add the sugar and mix on medium speed until combined.

Spread the mixture over the cooled pie and refrigerate until ready to serve.

Lingo

Cutting butter into flour is not difficult, but it takes a while. Hold two knives crisscrossed in the bowl and pull them apart repeatedly, cutting the butter into small pieces and incorporating the flour into the butter. The butter needs to be cold so it doesn't get completely incorporated into the flour. The little pieces of butter are what will make the pie crust flaky. Mixing more after the little pieces are coated with flour just makes the crust tough. If you have a food processor, you can put in the flour, salt, and butter and pulse a few times until small pea-sized, flour-coated pieces form. Then add the water and pulse until it just begins to hold together.

Baking the empty crust is called "blind baking." Because there are no ingredients in the crust, you have to add some type of weight to keep it from bubbling up. You can buy packages of little ceramic balls called pie crust weights (clever name, huh?), but dried beans or rice work just as well and are much cheaper. Once they've cooled off, you can put them back in the bag and use them over and over again.

BROWNIES

Megan

I think we should make brownies the official food ambassador around the world. Everyone likes brownies, they bring people together, and they even encourage non-bakers to bake! I have made brownies all over the world for people of many different nations, and no matter what was being discussed or debated before they tried them, once they got one of these brownies into their mouths, they stopped, paused a minute, and then smiled. The conversation never seems to get as heated again after brownies.

Cooking spray

4 oz/115 g unsweetened chocolate

1 cup/225 g butter

2 cups/400 g sugar

2 tsp vanilla extract

4 large eggs

1 cup/115 g all-purpose/plain flour

1 tsp baking powder

Preheat the oven to 350°F/180°C/gas mark 4. Coat a 9-by-13-inch/23-by-32-cm baking dish with cooking spray or oil.

Break each piece of chocolate into four pieces and put them all in a large microwave-safe bowl with the butter. Cook on high heat for 2 minutes and stir until smooth. Stir in the sugar and vanilla. Add the eggs one at a time, stirring well after each addition. Add the flour and baking powder and stir until just combined. Pour the batter into the prepared pan and bake for 30 minutes, until a toothpick inserted in the center comes out clean. Cool completely before cutting.

Ingredient Info

Baking powder and baking soda, also called bicarbonate of soda, are both leaveners, but they cannot be used interchangeably. Baking soda is used when there are acidic ingredients such as buttermilk or molasses/treacle. Baking powder is a combination of baking soda, cream of tartar, and cornstarch/cornflour, and it needs liquid to cause the chemical reaction. If you're out of baking powder you can use ¼ tsp baking soda and ½ tsp cream of tartar for every 1 tsp of baking powder in the recipe. If you're out of baking soda . . . go buy some more.

RASPBERRY SHORTBREAD BARS

Megan

Shortbread cookies/biscuits are light, buttery, and luscious, so it stands to reason that they're even more tasty with a little raspberry jelly sandwiched between the layers. You can make these with any kind of jelly, but raspberry is my favorite because it is sweet but tart. I know they say it about potato chips, but it's true for these bars too—no one can eat just one. You can make these bars with all-purpose/plain flour, but the cake/soft-wheat flour makes them so light they melt in your mouth.

1 cup/225 g butter, at room temperature

½ cup/50 g confectioners'/icing sugar

2 tsp vanilla extract

2½ cups/285 g cake/soft-wheat flour

1 cup/240 ml raspberry preserves

Preheat the oven to 325°F/165°C/gas mark 3.

Put the butter and sugar in a large bowl and mix with an electric mixer on low speed for 1 minute, or until the sugar is completely incorporated. Add the vanilla and mix on medium speed for 30 seconds. Add the flour and mix on low speed for 2 minutes, or until completely combined.

Put half of the dough in an 8- or 9-in/20- or 23-cm square baking pan/tin and press gently to cover the entire bottom of the pan. Spread the preserves evenly over the dough. Pull off small pieces of the remaining dough and drop them into the pan, loosely covering most of the preserves. (It's okay if some of the preserves are showing, but don't pat down the top layer of dough.) Bake for 35 to 40 minutes, or until lightly browned. Cool for 15 minutes and then cut into twenty bars.

CHOCOLATE CHIP COOKIES

Megan

Chocolate chip cookies/biscuits scream "home" to me. I still remember one of my first years at band camp (yes, I went to band camp), and I was getting a little home-sick when I got a big tin of chocolate chip cookies in the mail from my mom. That took care of the homesickness and made me a few new friends, too. I still love them, but my new favorite way to serve them is as the Pizza Cookies variation pictured here. It's a warm chocolate chip cookie, ice cream, and a bunch of spoons—still a good way to make friends!

1 cup/225 g butter, at room temperature

¾ cup/150 g granulated sugar

¾ cup/150 g firmly packed brown sugar

1 tsp vanilla extract

2 large eggs

1 tsp baking soda/ bicarbonate of soda

2½ cups/315 g flour

2 cups/340 g chocolate chips

Preheat the oven to 350°F/180°C/gas mark 4.

Put the butter, granulated sugar, and brown sugar in a large bowl and mix with an electric mixer on low speed for 1 minute, or until combined. Turn to medium speed and mix for 1 minute. Add the vanilla and eggs and mix on medium speed until completely incorporated. Add the baking soda/bicarbonate of soda and flour and mix on low speed for 2 minutes, or until combined. Add the chocolate chips and mix for 30 seconds, or until evenly distributed.

Drop heaping teaspoonfuls of the dough about 2 in/5 cm apart onto an ungreased baking sheet/tray and bake for 12 minutes, or until browned on the edges and the tops look dry. Remove the cookies/biscuits from the tray immediately and put them on cooling racks or waxed/greaseproof paper to cool. Repeat with the remaining dough.

·variation· PIZZA COOKIES

Mix the cookies as directed. Press the dough into two 8-in/20-cm round cake pans/tins and bake for 20 minutes. The cookies will be slightly underdone. Remove the pans from the oven, place several scoops of vanilla ice cream in the center of each cookie/ biscuit, and serve immediately.

Ingredient Info

Brown sugar can become hard even when it's stored in an airtight container. Adding a piece of bread to the container will soften the brown sugar again, but it takes a day or so. If you need to soften some right away, break it into chunks and put them in the microwave for 30 seconds. If it's really hard, it may need more time; just be sure to watch it carefully, or it will melt.

SUGAR COOKIES

Jill

The worst part about making cut-out cookies/biscuits is getting them to the baking sheet/tray intact. When I heard the tip about rolling the dough on parchment/baking paper and then pulling away the excess, I thought it was brilliant. Just make sure to leave enough space between the cookies to get to the dough. If the whole rolling thing is beyond you, drop the dough onto the baking sheet/tray and press it down with a glass dipped in sugar. Round versions taste good, too.

COOKIES/BISCUITS

¾ cup/170 g butter, at room temperature

1 cup/200 g sugar

2 large eggs

1 tsp vanilla extract

1 tsp baking powder

½ tsp salt

2½ cups/315 g all-purpose/plain flour

ICING

¼ cup/55 g butter, at room temperature

3 cups/300 g confectioners'/icing sugar

2 tbsp milk

Colored sugar, for decorating (optional)

To make the cookies/biscuits: Put the butter and sugar in a large bowl and mix with an electric mixer on low speed until completely combined. Add the eggs and vanilla and mix on medium speed for 1 minute, or until completely incorporated. Add the baking powder and salt and mix on medium speed until combined. Add the flour and mix on low speed until incorporated and then turn the mixer to medium and mix for 1 minute, or until smooth. Refrigerate the dough in the bowl for 1 hour.

Preheat the oven to 400°F/200°C/gas mark 6.

Cut two sheets of parchment/baking paper the size of a baking sheet/tray. Roll one-quarter of the dough out ⅛ to ¼ in/3 to 6 mm thick on the paper. Cut out shapes using cookie cutters, keeping the shapes ½ in/6 mm apart from each other to allow for spreading in the oven. Peel away the excess dough and put the paper on the baking sheet/tray. Bake for 6 to 8 minutes, or until lightly browned on the edges. Remove the cookies/biscuits from the paper and let them cool completely on a cooling rack. Repeat with the scraps and the remaining dough.

To make the icing: Put the butter in a bowl and mix with an electric mixer on medium speed until smooth. Add the sugar and milk and mix on low speed until incorporated. Turn the mixer to medium speed and mix for 1 minute, or until smooth.

Spread the icing over the cookies/biscuits and decorate with colored sugars, if desired. Let the icing dry completely before stacking them in an airtight container.

Ingredient Info

A can of baking powder can last a long time, but that's not always a good thing. If it loses its zip, your baked goods will end up flat as a pancake. To tell if your baking powder is still fresh, add 1 tsp of it to a cup of hot water. If it bubbles vigorously, it's good. If not, it's time to buy a new can.

MOLASSES COOKIES

Jill

I'll tell you right now that there's a problem with this recipe. You're supposed to refrigerate the dough for two hours before baking so it's not sticky. That doesn't work for me. If I'm making cookies/biscuits, it's because I want them now, not in two hours. So I drop the pieces of dough right into the sugar, shake the bowl around a little to get them covered, and then roll them into balls. Your hands get a little messier, but the instant gratification makes it well worth it.

1 cup/200 g sugar, plus extra for rolling

¾ cup/170 g butter, at room temperature

1 egg

¼ cup/60 ml molasses/treacle

2 tsp baking soda/bicarbonate of soda

1 tsp ground cinnamon

½ tsp ground cloves

½ tsp ground ginger

½ tsp salt

2 cups/255 g all-purpose/plain flour

Cooking spray

Put the 1 cup/ 200g sugar, butter, and egg in a large bowl and mix with an electric mixer on low speed for 1 minute, or until the ingredients are combined. Turn the mixer to high speed and mix for 1 minute, or until completely smooth. Add the molasses/ treacle, baking soda/bicarbonate of soda, cinnamon, cloves, ginger, and salt and mix on medium speed for 1 minute, or until combined. Add the flour and mix on low speed for 30 seconds, then turn the mixer to medium speed and mix until completely incorporated. Refrigerate the dough in the bowl for 2 hours or until completely chilled.

Preheat the oven to 375°F/190°C/gas mark 5. Lightly oil or coat a baking sheet/tray with cooking spray.

Put some sugar in a shallow bowl. Roll the dough into balls 1 in/ 2.5 cm in diameter and roll them in the sugar. Put the balls 2 in/ 5 cm apart on the prepared baking sheet/tray and bake for 8 minutes, or until the tops are cracked and the edges are set. Cool on the pan for 5 minutes and then remove the cookies/biscuits to parchment/baking paper or waxed/greaseproof paper to finish cooling.

INDEX

191